SATAN'S TRAP

*Twenty-Seven Years
in the Occult to Conversion*

by
ROB MILLER

Printed in the United States of America by
Graphic Connections Publishing
Chesterfield, Missouri 63005

DEDICATION

To

Our Blessed Mother

My late mother Norma Miller and my late father Bud Miller

My loving wife and son

CONTENTS

PART 2: The Occult and Demonic Explained

ACKNOWLEDGMENTS

Father Peter Mary Rookey, OSM

Our Lady of Lourdes

Betty G., Bob, and Son

Everyone at the Catholic Renewal Center

Anne, Jane, and Sister Charlotte

Father John, Father Ed, and Father Norb

Jesus and, of course, Our Heavenly Mother!

May I say to all of you, many thanks!!

ROB MILLER

INTRODUCTION

"He who does not believe in the devil does not believe in the Gospel."

St. Pope John Paul II

What you are about to read is absolutely true.

For some twenty-seven of my forty-eight years, I was deeply involved in the occult. My involvement consisted of a wide variety of different practices, including witchcraft, Voudon or Voodoo, Santería, Palo Mayombe, high magic, plus more.

Despite the warning from my father that "the good Lord can strike you dead for messing with that stuff," I ignored the warning and started reading tarot cards at age twelve. This in turn led to a barrage of occult practices spanning the next two decades, most of which I document in this book. Although not obeying my father's warning didn't leave me physically dead (it was, however, close), in essence it did kill me spiritually.

I now feel the need to inform the public about the dangers of such practices. Not only are the practices spiritually devastating, but they are a direct pipeline to the evil one and can also be physically and mentally harmful as well.

By the time I was an adult, I was doing readings for other people and was also was one of the youngest psychics to ever give readings at psychic fairs in the St. Louis area. During that period I began practicing Spiritualism and spirit communication. I then started to do public séances at the psychic fairs in addition to giving readings. At the same time I was delving deeper and deeper into the occult and magic.

I would eventually gain such a large following that it allowed me to open my first occult/new age bookstore. I ultimately owned two of these types of stores.

Little did I know that my occult practices would almost kill me. As a result of these practices I discovered that the occult is a direct pipeline to the demonic and the evil one (Satan). Of course, I'd heard from the preachers and ministers about the dangers of the occult, most of which I thought of as pure nonsense. Despite this I still continued to dabble with the devil and his minions.

I had even developed a somewhat hatred for Christianity and Christians. To most occultists and me, Christians were hypocrites and the enemy. We thought of the preachers and ministers who criticized the occult as being hypocritical and small minded. "I'm not consorting with the devil. I'm channeling angels, and my powers and abilities come from God!" I thought. There are still some psychics that try to justify their abilities by convincing themselves that these abilities come from God! How wrong that thought is!

What I encountered over the last few months of my involvement in the occult was pure evil! This led me to the realization that Satan and his demons do exist and that they aren't merely a figment of superstitious Christian belief. These evil deities are constantly tempting Christians in the hopes of stealing them from Jesus, as Satan and his minions hate humanity. There are many temptations, but the one Satan loves the most is the occult as it remains the most offensive to God. As I discovered that Satan and the demonic were real, then I thought there must be a Jesus. Jesus and the intervention of the Blessed Mother are what saved me from the brink of death.

My story is one of healing, some of which my family and I are still doing.

I have broken this book down into two parts. The first part is my personal story. In the second part, I've tried to compile everything I know on the demonic and occult that I felt would be helpful. This section includes information as well as prayers. Most useful is the section on spells and curses—how they work and prayers for getting rid of them—as well as the section on occult religions.

There seems to be a lack of this type of material available to the Catholic public. To be quite frank, this is the stuff people hardly ever discuss in public for fear of ridicule.

Occult practitioners and the evil one certainly won't like this book as I give away several secrets usually only known to practitioners. For privacy purposes, I've changed names of people, locations, and groups. I've changed some of the times of incidents as well.

I sincerely hope this book makes some people think twice before dabbling in the occult. The seemingly most innocent of things connected to the occult, if practiced, can end with horrible consequences.

I recommend that you pray the Prayer of Saint Michael before reading this book, just as a precaution. You can find the prayer in chapter 26.

If this book helps only one person think twice before dabbling in the occult, then it will have served its purpose.

With love in Christ and Mary,

Rob Miller

PART 1

MY STORY

CHAPTER 1

MEXICO AND THE WITCHES CORNER

"My dear children, be on your guard. The devil will tempt you with bad books, bad thoughts, or the foul conversation of a companion."

Saint John Bosco

I didn't grow up in an overly religious atmosphere. While my parents said we were Presbyterian, I had never attended church nor was I ever baptized. Not being baptized was one of the reasons the evil one had such a tight and long hold on me. My parents believed in God; it's just that we never went to church. I would later find that while growing up my father seemed to have a deeper faith than my mother. Later in life my father would purchase several dozen rosaries from a man who handcrafted them although we were not Catholic. His reasoning for purchasing them was that the man was out of work and needed the money. Whether my father actually prayed with them, I'll never know.

I was later told by my mother that my father accompanied a priest who was a friend of his on several instances to southern Missouri in an effort to get a parishioner's child out of some type of cult. To the best of my knowledge this cult was not related to the occult, and the attempts were unsuccessful.

I was born and grew up in North St. Louis in a suburb called Normandy long before it became crime ridden. For the most part my neighborhood was the typical 1970s neighborhood.

My grandmother lived across the street from us. I was very close to my grandmother, and my parents allowed me to stay at her house most of the time. Now that I look back on it, it was probably due to my father's drinking problem. My mother probably felt I was safer there than at home when my father drank.

I was also very close to my mother. Around my teenage years I would discover that my mother had a long history of patronizing psychics, mediums, and spiritualists. I would also discover that most of my aunts on my mother's side were heavy into Spiritualism, as was my great-grandmother. In their younger years they would constantly use a Ouija board as well as hold séances. This was all except for my aunt Goldie, who I called Gome for short. She was a devout Catholic who at one time worked as a cook for nuns in a convent.

My father was a hydraulic repairman and owned his own business. My mother was a secretary, and my grandmother was retired from McDonnell Douglas.

I attended Bel-Nor elementary and for the most part was a good student.

As a child, I had three experiences with the occult.

The first experience was when our neighbor Mrs. Mosely moved out. Mrs. Mosely rented her home out to a couple in their mid-twenties. The young couple had a large black Lab dog as well as a German shepherd. The black Lab's name was Satan. Of course, not going to church, I had no idea who or what Satan was. I would spend many a day calling out to the dog from my side of the fence, "Here, Satan, come here." At night we could hear strange chanting coming from the home, especially on weekends. There was always a crowd at their home on these days. Looking back, I now believe these people were likely Satanists.

I was intrigued about ghosts and the supernatural. My friend Jim Nelson and I would constantly check out books from the library on this material as well as participate in long discussions about it.

My second pre-teen experience with the occult occurred on a family trip to Mexico without my father. During this trip, my mother, grandmother, and I visited Mexico City, Acapulco, the Shrine of Guadalupe, and the Mexican pyramids. I found the Shrine of Guadalupe uplifting even at such a young age. I still remember people walking on their knees around the shrine on concrete.

After visiting the pyramids of the sun and moon, we went shopping at a Mexican market. At that time, jumping beans were a big fad item in Mexico, and I wanted some. (Just for your information, these actually exist and are small beans that contain an insect that causes them to jump.) I visited one of the stores in the market looking for the jumping beans. This particular store had the beans as well as candles in various shapes, such as men, women, etc. They also featured a large number of statues, plants, and herbs. I would later discover that this store was actually a botanica, or Santería shop.

When I paid the man for the beans (I had my own stack of pesos), he looked at my mother and said, "Your son is very spiritual. He will eventually foretell the future!" I remember this clearly. My mother nodded for whatever reason, then we left, never to speak of the incident again. Looking back, it may have just been a sales pitch to try to sell us some type of psychic potion or something, but it was still a strange thing to hear.

My third pre-teen occult experience occurred at about age eleven.

During the summertime, once a week my mother and grandmother would drag me to the beauty shop with them while my father was working.

Bored out of my skull one day while waiting for them to finish at the beauty shop, I glanced out the front window and noticed a strange store across the street.

The store was named Witches Corner, and it was one of the oldest occult bookstores in the Midwest. When I say occult, I mean *occult*! No cheesy new age stuff there, only hard-core occultism. Anyone who was anyone in the occult scene in the Midwest went to Witches Corner. Some famous occultists would even stop by on their way through while traveling.

Witches Corner was run by an older gentleman named Bill. Bill was in his mid-fifties with a gray beard and glasses. Bill had the appearance of being a loving grandfather type, but looks can be deceiving. Bill told the general public he was into ghost hunting but, in all actuality, he was into dark traditional witchcraft as well as dark ritual magic.

Rumor had it that during the Satanic Panic of the 1980s, Witches Corner was under heavy surveillance by federal and local law enforcement agencies looking for Satanists. During this time due to several talk shows like *Geraldo*, there was a widespread fear of satanic cults. There were heavy rumors that satanic cults were kidnapping and killing children after sexually abusing them. Most of this was pure nonsense. But the rumor was compounded by the fact that Michael Aquino, founder of the satanic Temple of Set, had recently moved to south St. Louis from San Francisco. Aquino was a regular patron of Witches Corner. There were always recruiting posters for the Temple of Set on the store's community bulletin board.

One police officer from North County even went so far as to say that the entire worldwide headquarters for traditional witchcraft was run out of a backroom at Witches Corner. The same police officer also claimed to have Michael Aquino's residence in south St. Louis under constant surveillance.

I would always go over to Witches Corner while my mother and grandmother were at the beauty shop. It began to be a regular thing. They never said anything, as when my mother went over to Witches Corner to pick me up when they were done, she would always exchange subtle greetings with Bill and ask him if he knew of any new psychics. My mother had a strong interest in psychics.

Bill tolerated me for whatever reason. He would always ask me how my mother was. I would spend my allowance on occult books. These I kept hidden from my father.

Witches Corner had a certain energy about it. Even the scent of the incense and herbs would almost pull you in. I later discovered that when business was slow, Bill would perform money drawing rituals in the back room. This may explain why I was so attracted to it.

There was an old printing press in the back room that he used to start his own occult publishing company. Bill published witchcraft books most often, as he had an arrangement of sorts with two famous witches to publish their works.

Little did I know my relationship with Bill would grow into a lifelong friendship until we had a falling out when I opened my first occult bookstore.

According to occult lore, when someone starts to seriously delve into the dark occult arts, they usually give up something (or rather the devil takes it away). This something that is usually given up appears in the form of mental or physical illness as well as suffering. Of course, I now know how this works, as it's the devil causing these illnesses in exchange for whatever the intended goal was in your ritual work. Also, when the devil does give you something, there is always something wrong with it or the positive change is only temporary. When you make a deal with the devil (even by performing what seems to be the most innocent of rituals) he will always expect something in return. For some the illnesses are deadly, for others they last a lifetime. Mine has lasted nearly a lifetime.

Of course, I wasn't really aware at such a young age that what Bill taught me during our friendship was dark magic. I was taught by Bill that magic was magic and there was no white magic nor black magic. The theory behind white magic and black magic is more or less taught in Wicca and Voodoo circles.

Shortly after I started becoming a regular fixture at Witches Corner, I started having vivid dreams. There was usually an elderly old hag of a woman stirring a pot and giving me an evil look. It was during this time that I developed obsessive-compulsive disorder (OCD for short). I would feel for whatever reason the unnerving need to count things. I would count ceiling tiles, the numbers on an alarm clock, etc. This disorder would later intensify during the last few months of my occult practices. (You'll read about that later.) It's now almost fully treated although I do still take a small amount of medication for it and have been gradually cutting down the medication over the last few years. I believe the OCD was caused by the devil in exchange for success at the ritual work Bill was teaching me.

It wasn't long after the dreams began that I would wake up in the middle of the night after having a dream that the old hag was sitting on my chest. I would awaken from this dream finding nothing there, but it felt like there was an elephant sitting on my chest. This occurred at least two times per week.

During one of my visits to Witches Corner, I asked Bill what to do about the old hag and the dreams. Bill said that the old hag was actually a succubus spirit and that I should perform a banishing ritual the next time it happened. The ritual worked; however, when

I would later do ritual work with a scrying mirror, I would still see the old hag in the mirror.

It was during these early teenage years that our neighborhood started to decline into a crime-ridden area. My mother returned home one day after her job as school secretary and told my father that the principal had caught a third grader with a switchblade. My father, mother, and grandmother decided it was time to sell their homes and leave town for my best interest.

We then moved to Farmington, Missouri, a small town about seventy miles south of St. Louis.

CHAPTER 2

TAROT CARDS, SPIRITS, AND THE ROOT LADY

"If a person turns to mediums and necromancers, whoring after them, I will set my face against that person and will cut them off from among his people."

Leviticus 20:6

So there I was, almost thirteen years old and living in a small rural community. This was a big adjustment for a kid from the city. With barely anything to do, I immersed myself in my occult practices.

I would look for and gather herbs for my rituals on a regular basis. After all, there were plenty of woods and wilderness areas.

I had already started to experiment with tarot cards. As I was limited to purchasing new stuff, I began an in-depth study with what I had. By then I was developing quite a library that I kept hidden from my father in the back of my closet. I had a deck of Rider-Waite tarot cards as well as a deck of Gypsy Witch fortune-telling cards. By now my mother would ask for me to give her readings on a regular basis whenever my father wasn't around. I eventually quit this as I didn't like to read family members, as I was too close to them.

What makes one a good reader is to study the artwork on each card closely. Some advanced ritual magicians study and meditate on one card for weeks. There are many types of tarot decks. One thing is for certain. The more you "study" the individual cards, the more the evil one has his hold on you.

Due to the lack of occult materials in Farmington, I dove headfirst into studying the tarot and became proficient at reading them.

When we moved to Farmington, my father sold his hydraulic business. He and my mother opened a small T-shirt printing business and gift shop. In order to pick up supplies for the business, my parents and I made regular trips to St. Louis and Memphis. Of course when those trips excluded my father, the trips to St. Louis would always include enticing my mother to stop at Witches Corner, and she always obliged.

The family business enabled me to contact Bill freely because the business phone bills almost always included calls to St. Louis, so my father never paid any attention.

By now, my taste of occult materials had deepened. I now wanted the more hard-core stuff like Aleister Crowley and the medieval ritual works of Éliphas Lévi.

One day I decided to test Bill on his knowledge of herbs. I had learned that Indian hemp was the old medicinal name for marijuana, so one day I asked Bill if he had any Indian hemp. His response, "You should have all kinds of pot down where you live now!" We both had a good laugh. Why he tolerated me I'll never know.

In Memphis, the suppliers were close to Beale Street. On one occasion after visiting her suppliers, my mother and I went shopping and looking around Beale Street.

We wandered into a store called General Mercantile. General Mercantile was an old-time general store. Their motto was, "If you can't find it at General Mercantile, then you don't need it!" This was essentially true because they carried nearly everything you could imagine from lead pipe to Budweiser hats. They also had a large section of Voodoo and Hoodoo supplies. This is where my next spiritual direction began to take shape, or as I should say, the evil one pointed me in this direction.

General Mercantile was nearly the only place in Memphis where the local community could purchase Voodoo and Hoodoo supplies, and apparently they did a brisk business. For those of you wondering the difference between Voodoo and Hoodoo, let me explain. Voodoo is an African religion, whereas Hoodoo uses the components such as herbs, incense, etc., without actually practicing the religious aspects of Voodoo.

The place was always packed in the Voodoo section, as I call it. It was there that I met a woman we'll call Desiree. Desiree was an older black lady with no children. She was in her midsixties. Desiree had an eerie resemblance to Marie Laveau, the New Orleans Voodoo queen. Desiree knew this and used it to her benefit whenever possible. Her skin was light brown, and she wore a bandanna on her head. Whenever I saw her, she was always wearing hoop earrings.

I met Desiree one day when I asked one of General Mercantile's employees if they knew of a good reader. Desiree, who was within earshot, spoke up and said, "I'm a root worker." My mother found this intriguing and immediately set up an appointment with Desiree. We followed Desiree back to her house after she made her purchases.

Desiree's house from the outside was simple: a small two-bedroom home that had dirty wooden siding that was once white. However, upon entering her home, my mother and I discovered it was immaculate. I could tell she was using incense on regular occasions because it permeated the air. Her living room consisted of a large console television, a recliner that looked like it had seen better days, and a sofa. She did her readings in the dining room, which was open to the living room. On the walls were shelves of herbs, as well as a Bible. There were things called Adam & Eve Root, High John the Conqueror, black cat bone, Triple Crown Incense, and cleansing floor wash.

Right before my mother's reading, there was a knock at the door. Desiree told the visitor to enter. A nicely dressed black man in his forties entered the room. Desiree instructed him to have a seat while she started reading my mother. I would later discover that Desiree was a pretty famous root worker and reader in the South. She would travel between Memphis and New Orleans, where she owned another small home.

Desiree started to give my mother her reading. My mother was seated across from Desiree at the table while I sat in the living room on the sofa by the nicely dressed man. He gave me a nod so I returned it.

I listened intently to my mother's reading because this was all new to me and it all was intriguing.

Desiree had my mother reach into a bowl and pick up some herbs and roots, then drop them on the table. I noticed that this was similar to the way tea leaves are read. Then Desiree started to speak.

"Who's Bob or Bud? He's very close to you; his name begins with a B?"

"Bud is my husband's nickname," my mother responded, surprised.

My mouth dropped and I thought to myself, "How in the heck did she just pull my father's nickname out of thin air?" I intently listened for more.

"My dear, your husband drinks too much ... it's going to make him very sick, you know this?" Desiree asked.

"Yes," my mother responded.

Holy Toledo! I said to myself. She just picked up on my father's drinking and pulled it right out of thin air as well. Needless to say the reading continued, and Desiree continued to hit right on the mark! She said I would be driving a new red car when I was of age to get my driver's license. She also picked up on my occult practices.

"Your son is into the spiritual, but he has a teacher that isn't good for him. He will go far and predict the future just as I, but he must get rid of this man first," Desiree said.

After it was over, she asked my mother to open the Bible to any section. Desiree closed her eyes and pointed to something in the open Bible. She proceeded to tie the Bible verse in with the reading. She then handed my mother the cassette tape of the reading with one of her business cards. We thanked her and left.

I knew Desiree was referring to Bill as my teacher. I made the decision to limit, but not totally isolate, my visits to Bill and the Witches Corner.

After about three visits to Desiree at various times, she sort of took me under her wing (at my persistence and begging) and agreed to be my new teacher.

There were two things that my mother loved as her pastimes. One was bingo and the other was psychics. On future trips to Memphis, when Desiree wasn't in New Orleans, my mother would get her reading from Desiree, then leave me with Desiree while she drove a couple of blocks to an evening bingo game. This lasted a few hours, and that gave me plenty of time to get to know Desiree and learn from her.

Desiree claimed to have learned how to work the roots from her grandmother. Although Desiree had Catholic statues in her home, she was a devout Spiritualist and claimed her powers and abilities were given to her by God. This of course is a crock of lies, as the Bible distinctly warns against mediums.

Spiritualist church services usually include a séance in which psychic messages are given to the parishioners by the medium. I attended several Spiritualist church services over the years with Desiree.

I never asked about the Catholic saint statues because I already knew the answer. Desiree also practiced Voodoo, and that's why she had the statues. Long ago statues of Catholic saints were used by African slaves who wanted to disguise their Voodoo religion from their slave masters who were Catholics. The slaves assigned a Voodoo god or deity to a Catholic saint. They then could openly practice their Voodoo in the presence of the slave masters who thought they were practicing Catholicism. This is why there are usually Catholic statues found on or around Voodoo practitioners. This practice carries into Santería and other Congo religions as well. From a religious Catholic standpoint, it is total bastardization of the holy saints. This is one factor that the devil thoroughly enjoys, and that's why ritual practices of African-style occult religions work quickly and are dangerous.

From Desiree, I learned a ton of things. The rituals she taught were simple but worked quickly and were powerful. More power, in fact, than I was used to working with. I learned the roots as well as mediumship, or what is more commonly known in new age circles as "channeling." Desiree would always call me "child." She would only call me by my actual name when she was frustrated with me or angry.

I began seeing a vision of an old black man. His name was Haji. I started to channel Haji, and he would give messages or sometimes whole readings to those listening. Haji's actual last name was Glapion, and he was one of Marie Laveau's lovers.

Haji gave us all sorts of facts about his life, most of which I verified by doing research.

So there I was, only fifteen and a half years old and that far advanced in the occult.

It was during this time that my grandmother was diagnosed with lung cancer that spread to her brain. She passed quickly. This was devastating to me. Shortly thereafter, just as Desiree said, my father developed emphysema and pancreatic cancer. He stopped drinking alcohol and turned to Diet 7UP.

My father then started to collect more Catholic items just like the rosaries he had previously purchased. He ordered and started carrying a small crucifix that contained water from Lourdes.

It was about this time that my father caught me with an occult book entitled *Voodoo Handbook of Cult Secrets* by Anna Riva. He destroyed the book and told me that the good Lord would strike me dead for messing with that stuff! My mother looked at me with a raised eyebrow and kind of rolled her eyes. My father didn't know the extent of our psychic visits.

When I turned sixteen my parents bought me a 1976 Chevy Nova with the shift on the column. I hated that car. One morning on the way to school, the thing died on me right in front of the courthouse. I managed to push it over to the side of the road and began kicking the driver's side door. One of my father's friends must have seen this as it wasn't too much longer until I was the happy owner of a brand-new Chevy Cavalier in what other color but candy-apple red, just as Desiree had predicted.

It was shortly after my father had his teeth pulled that he turned completely jaundiced. After being rushed to the hospital, we were told that the cancer had reached a terminal stage. My father asked to be put into a VA hospital in Poplar Bluff, Missouri. He said he thought that they may be able to help him. However, I think that the real reason for his wanting to go there was because he didn't want to leave the burden of a large hospital bill on us. He was entitled to stay there after his service in World War II.

During this time, one of my mother's friends suggested she start going to church. It was at the Nazarene church that we met Pastor Frank. My father was "saved" by Pastor Frank, and Pastor Frank made repeated trips all the way to Poplar Bluff to visit my father before his passing. My mother and I were touched by this and the church's kindness. We started going to the Nazarene church frequently. The youth minister named Charles took me fishing once. He asked me to bring along all of my occult paraphernalia so we could destroy it. He destroyed the items in the river.

I, of course, didn't turn over everything. I did keep a few of my most prized occult possessions.

My mother and I then asked about joining the Nazarene church. Pastor Frank told us we couldn't be accepted because we both smoked and my mother played bingo. This was hard for me to understand because they were compassionate toward my father. It was this act that turned me further against Christianity as a whole and pushed me further into my occult practices. I was glad I didn't let Charles destroy everything. Although I was "saved" in the Nazarene church, this meant absolutely nothing to me after what happened. I dove straight back into the occult.

CHAPTER 3

DEMONS, OUIJA BOARDS, AND THE INITIATION

*"Thou didst hate for their detestable practices,
their works of sorcery and unholy rites."*

Wisdom 12:4

After my father's death, I no longer had to hide my practices. I started doing psychic fairs in the St. Louis area. I became acquainted with almost everyone in the St. Louis occult community.

As my mother had to run the business with only me, we saw less and less of Desiree as we didn't go to Memphis often. My mother actually found a psychic in Farmington. Her name was Janet, and she read with the Gypsy fortune-telling deck. Janet didn't actually live in Farmington but would travel from St. Louis once a week. She would do readings at a person named Liz's home.

When Janet wasn't there, Liz would invite my mother and me over for Ouija board sessions. My mother started to use the Ouija board. I purchased one for my mother and me to use. One night some friends of mine were using the board. We harped on our friend Tom to use the board. Tom was hesitant as he was a devout Catholic. He did, and a spark flew off the pointer (planchette). This was a board from the 1980s, a typical Parker Brothers board. There was no metal absolutely anywhere on the board. Tom left, and we never discussed it again. I now know that the evil one was disrupted by Tom's faith in Jesus and Mary, so he sent a visible spark through the plastic pointer to back Tom off. A shocked Tom got up in a hurry and went into the other room, refusing to participate any further.

My practices started taking on a more ominous tone. I started practicing ritual magic. I later would attempt to summon demons using a certain occult book. With a little research, it's easy to conjure demons. The book itself lists various demons and their shapes but refers to them as angels and spirits. The book fails to list them as what they truly are: fallen angels. Although I knew the difference, this can be confusing to someone just getting into the occult. During these rituals, I would cast the magic circles. The demon would eventually manifest itself in one of the circles. Sometimes I would use a black scrying mirror (a mirror used to perform divination) to see the image. At other times I would put the incense burner there to allow the incense smoke to take the shape of the entity. Of course, there were words and incantations said during the invocation ritual.

The strange thing about invoking the demonic is that they may appear right away, in a week, a month, or maybe even a year, but they definitely will eventually show themselves in one form or another.

A typical amateur mistake is to fail to banish or send the demon back before closing the circle. As young as I was, I had no business messing around with a book like that. I failed to dismiss or banish the demon. I should mention at this time that these demons are usually invoked for cursing purposes to send to an enemy or to cause strife. However, each also has its own purpose such as wealth, lust, etc.

After the first few rituals, I quit when nothing immediately happened and closed the circle.

Several days later, I had a dream in which I saw a spirit that matched the book's description of the demon's appearance. The demon was calling my name out. Suddenly, I felt as though I was being strangled. When I opened my eyes, I was face to face with the succubus demon of the old hag I had previously only seen in my dreams. Although, this time, the entity's eyes were completely black, and it was sitting on my chest only a few inches from my face. I quickly remembered the banishing ritual Bill said to use, and the entity disappeared. Down the hall I heard a door slam; however, when I went to investigate, all the doors were wide open!

Most people at this stage of the game would have quit out of fear. However, I felt an overwhelming surge of excitement and power in that I had actually summoned an entity.

During the course of my ritual magic practices, the old hag would appear regularly in the scrying mirror or on my chest. Sometimes the eyes were pitch black, other times they were yellow.

I cleansed the entire house with a smudge stick regularly; however, the entity still remained. I finally called Bill about the matter. He said not to worry because the rituals in the book were more designed to get into your head. More than likely, the entity was nothing more than a negative thought form that would disappear in time.

Nonsense! I knew I had summoned something as I could sense its presence, and now this unwanted visitor wouldn't leave! The entity eventually left after a time when I remembered Desiree telling me to open a Bible to Psalm 46 in order to get rid of any unwanted ghost or spirit. I figured if it was good enough for ghosts, then why not an entity.

My mother continued to go over to Liz's and participate in the Ouija sessions. My mother would always try to contact my father or grandmother.

After one of these sessions, I had a dream in which my father and grandmother were standing at the foot of my bed smiling.

My father was holding our family dog Candy, who had recently disappeared. I told my mother about this. She seemed somewhat comforted. I believe this dream was significant because I firmly believe that these were their actual spirits visiting us to tell me and my mother that they were fine and there was no need to use the Ouija board anymore.

I continued to channel Haji while my mother or others took notes. Most of what Haji communicated was material pertaining to Voodoo. Of course, the spirit had his demands, which were rum and cigars. During one channeling sitting, I drank a pint of rum while under. When I came out of the sitting, I was totally sober. When I would go into these sessions, I would relax as Desiree taught me until I felt a tingling on my neck. I then felt as if I were out of my body, looking down on the session from above. When the spirit would enter, I would feel tingling in the hands as if after being shocked. Usually I would have little or no memory of the session at all.

I wanted to find other like-minded people, so I decided to put a small amount of occult stuff up for sale in the back of my mother's store. This worked perfectly as, within a month, I found several people who had an interest in traditional witchcraft. These were all adults over the age of eighteen, so I decided to start a witch's coven.

I initiated myself one evening. Our meetings consisted of a feast or dinner, then we would participate in a ritual circle. In the center of the circle, I had a large red trunk that served as an altar and I stored all of the coven's ritual supplies in it. Most of the work consisted of love and money spells. The coven's rituals worked with great success; however, there wasn't enough to sate my palate, so I still continued my ritual magic practices.

It was at one of these meetings that I met Dianne. Dianne was five years my senior. We started dating, and after a few months, she suggested I move in with her. Being young and stupid, I said yes.

Needless to say our relationship never worked out, so after a while I moved out.

There was one experience I had while living with her that told me she was into the occult deeper than I suspected. Our apartment was upstairs in an old Victorian-style house. I awoke one night because I heard the squeaking of the rocking chair rocking back and forth. At first I thought this was Dianne's four-year-old daughter, but after closer inspection, I noticed a glare coming off the head of whoever or whatever was sitting there. The glare appeared to be coming off a pair of horns. A goatlike creature with red eyes was staring back at me while rocking back and forth. When I got within about seven feet of the creature, it disappeared.

I thought that I truly loved Dianne, so I performed a love ritual to draw her to me. There's an old saying that goes "Be careful what you wish for ..."

About three weeks after I completed the ritual, Dianne started calling me. I had already met someone else and was moving on as we had a lot more in common.

Dianne persisted and called me several times per day. I couldn't get rid of her. Dianne continued to pursue me by claiming I was the father of her child and filing paternity suits against me. The DNA test showed I wasn't the father, but whenever she would move to a new state or county, she would file from there, so I'd get hit with another suit. Those involved in the occult, especially witchcraft, find special significance in the number three, and everything happens in threes. Finally, after three years she left me alone, but only after my spending three thousand dollars in legal fees.

This interval of threes exists in the occult because the evil one mocks the Holy Trinity of Father, Son, and Holy Spirit. In essence, things happen in threes when it pertains to the occult, as it's the devil's work.

CHAPTER 4

ASPEN AND BILL'S OFFER

"Nor a fortune-teller, soothsayer, charmer, diviner, or caster of spells,
nor one who consults ghosts and spirits or seeks oracles from the dead.
Anyone who does such things is an abomination to the Lord."

Deuteronomy 18:10–12

As I held the admissions forms in my hand, my mother's advice to me was simply, "There's another world out there besides Farmington. Go see it!"

Disappointed with the dead-end jobs available in Farmington and its surrounding areas, I now pointed my educational direction to a security training academy in Aspen, Colorado. This particular academy trained bodyguards or, as they referred to them, "executive protection specialists."

After a rather lengthy background investigation, psychological exam, and financial approval, my application was finally accepted. It wasn't long before I left for Aspen. I was twenty-one years old.

After completing my training, I soon went to work. Many of my first assignments were what is referred to as "strike work" in the security profession. This involved flying around the country and providing security during labor strikes, especially when those companies had vested interests with the federal government. During this time, I worked for a paper mill that manufactured treasury paper. Our job tilted more toward strike breaking than security.

I worked twelve-hour shifts, seven days per week, for a month at a time. Every other month, I was allowed to fly home, unless I preferred to stay. The pay was excellent and even included a per diem. When the strike was over, we simply went on to another assignment. When I went home, I would continue my occult practices.

My mother and I still continued to go to psychic fairs all over the United States. For those of you who don't know about psychic fairs, these are large gatherings of psychics and vendors of occult and new age materials. The events are usually held in hotel banquet rooms.

It wasn't long before I was selling at the fairs. After taking a test regarding my psychic abilities, I was allowed to do readings at the fairs. I eventually went all over the Midwest doing psychic fairs, except when working security.

One particular promoter named Cheryl promoted a fair that held public séances. Cheryl told me she was in a tight jam, as her medium that normally did the séances couldn't do them for some reason. She asked me if I could do them. I then held my first public séance.

The séances were a huge success. One evening, I had to do two extra séances due to the high demand. At each séance, there were about seventy-five to one hundred people in attendance.

The séances worked as follows. The first thing I did was channel Haji, my spirit guide. Haji would then, in turn, call out people's names and they would stand and he would deliver the messages to them from the departed. Needless to say this was rather exhausting.

The final séance I did for Cheryl went terribly. As was customary at every séance, I warned the audience about arguing with the spirits; however, this particular audience wouldn't listen. When I brought Haji through to start delivering messages, the audience members started to argue with the departed, saying things like you owed me money, you were having an affair with my wife, etc. The whole thing was terribly negative. At least, this is the report I got after coming out from under the trance state.

When I finally came out of my trance state, my right hand hurt intensely. It appears that Haji or something had placed my hand into hot candle wax during the last portion of the séance. My hand remained in the wax for at least ten minutes. I went to the emergency room and was treated for a second-degree burn on the right hand. Remarkably, it healed completely with no scarring.

Needless to say, and despite Cheryl's asking me to do more, this was my last public séance. I still, however, continued to channel Haji during private readings.

It was also during this time that I met my wife, Cathy. Cathy was a client of mine at the fairs. We hit it off and after a year we decided to move in together. We lived in a two-bedroom apartment in south St. Louis.

On one occasion, I took Cathy to Witches Corner and introduced her to Bill. Bill wasn't happy about me doing psychic fairs. He claimed that all of the St. Louis psychics got their start by buying materials from Witches Corner and when they made a steady income, the psychics stopped coming in and were saying Bill was evil.

Because Bill's place was the only show in town for several years, it attracted people of all occult beliefs, including Satanists, witches, Wiccans, etc. Rumors still lurked regarding how Bill's store was supposed to be under surveillance by law enforcement. Most of the St. Louis psychics wanted no part of this.

A reserve cop even went so far as to say that the entire satanic and witchcraft movement was run out of the back room of Witches Corner. This was a load of nonsense. I've been in the backroom. All that was there was a desk and some old bags of trash.

Bill offered me a proposition that I wanted to take advantage of at that time. He offered Witches Corner to me and Cathy lock, stock, and barrel for $40,000. He even offered to finance part of the transaction himself. If I had the money, we may have bought it, but we didn't have the down payment.

Now that I look back, I was probably better off without it as I knew Bill was becoming heavily involved with some satanic groups that I won't mention here.

Little did I know that Bill's offer to me would ruin our friendship.

CHAPTER 5

OUR NEW STORE AND THE APARTMENT

"Whatever the less discerning theologians may say, the devil, as far as Christian belief is concerned, is a puzzling but real, personal, and not merely symbolic presence."

Pope Benedict XVI

By mid-1992, I had been saving money but still didn't have enough cash for Bill's down payment. I did, however, have enough to open my own small store.

Cathy and I went hunting for a space to lease. We found a great deal. The deal consisted of a seven-hundred-square-foot store front plus a two-bedroom apartment all for only five hundred dollars per month. The property was located in south St. Louis.

When I first went upstairs to look at the apartment I almost backed out. The place had a weird feeling about it that I can only describe as a "dirty vibe." I never said anything to Cathy, but I got the feeling someone had died a horrible death there. I also thought I felt a dark presence but shrugged it off. The deal was too good to pass up, so we took it.

A month later, we moved into the apartment and began working on the store. We did most of the work ourselves in order to save money.

I made sure I put the word "botanica" in the name to cater to anyone in the Santería religion. I added "in the New Orleans tradition" to cater to anyone involved in the religion of Voodoo and its counterparts. I wanted to cater to those who were serious about their occult beliefs, as they were the ones who would spend the most money. I carried incense, oils, candles, herbs, and a few books. These were the essentials of any good occult supply shop. I sent out mailers from my list of clients announcing the opening of my new store.

Within another month, we opened for business. Our opening was a huge success; however, there was someone who wasn't that happy, and that someone was Bill.

Within a couple of weeks of our opening, Bill and his latest lady friend paid me a visit one afternoon. Bill wanted to know why I hadn't purchased his store instead of opening my own. I told him about the $15,000 difference between my own store cost and his required down payment. He said he felt betrayed. Bill was probably feeling pressured, as another person who used to do psychic fairs opened their store at the same time I did.

Bill was in no mood to discuss the matter. He insinuated that I was telling my clients that he and his store were evil, which I absolutely didn't do. Bill also said I was no better than the rest of the other psychics who wanted nothing to do with him anymore!

I tried my best to explain to Bill that these were mostly rumors that had been circulating about his shop for years. Bill finally threatened me by saying he was going to dust his altar off and teach me a lesson! This really ticked me off. I felt it was totally unjustified. I also considered how bull-headed Bill could be.

Later, after they left, I called Bill at Witches Corner. I told him that I was willing to send letters out on our behalf to my clientele, asking them to patronize both stores and informing them of the incident. Naturally, he refused and said to forget the whole thing.

Two days later, I went downstairs to open the shop and discovered that the place had a strange feeling about it. I soon discovered that both of the iguanas (we had two in a cage on the counter) were dead. All of the fish in the shop's aquarium were also dead. A few hours later, my mother called and told me that my dog, which was still with her in Farmington, was having some type of seizures and she needed to be taken to the vet.

This was too much of a coincidence all to happen at the same time. I thought of Bill's threat and chalked this up to a witchcraft-style curse.

I started to smudge (a Native American form of cleansing). After smudging the place free of negative energies (or so I thought), I went to work on the second phase, which included performing a ritual to send back all of the negative energy to whoever had sent it. Although I highly suspected Bill, I couldn't be certain, so therefore, I performed the ritual as described above.

The ritual worked all too well. The store had a cleansed air about it. Now all I had to do was wait to see what would happen to the person who had sent the curse, for then I'd find my culprit.

As I waited for something to happen, I met Gator and Lydia. These two people drove all the way from Kentucky to come to my shop. Gator had a big interest in root work and Voodoo as well. He wanted to become my understudy.

Gator was one of the most humorous people I'd ever met. I took an instant liking to these two, as did Cathy. Instead of staying at a hotel, I suggested they stay with us in the extra bedroom, and they were thankful and obliged. This would become a regular practice when they came up from Kentucky.

Gator was tall and had a wiry frame, and Lydia was fifteen years Gator's senior. But I didn't mind, as I thought of the two as old souls.

One evening I decided to hold a channeling session for Gator and Lydia with Haji. They observed while Cathy took notes. After coming out of a trance, I discovered that Haji said he had a couple of gifts for me. He kept repeating the words "mad hatter" over and over. This stumped me for some time, as I didn't have a clue as to what he was talking about. The only Mad Hatter I knew of was from the children's story *Alice's Adventures in Wonderland*.

This continued to bother me for over a week. I would see visions of the Mad Hatter from the children's story in my dreams. Finally, I decided to see if maybe the Mad Hatter was a place, so I called information. There was a Mad Hatter Antiques store located on Cherokee Street in St. Louis City. I knew that had to be it, so the following weekend, we all piled in the car and went to Cherokee Street.

When we arrived at the Mad Hatter Antiques shop, we discovered an authentic Voodoo drum hand carved from the trunk of a tree. We also found an old Voodoo altar bottle. This was wrapped in cypress and used for going from house to house when performing rituals. There were two faces, one on each side of the bottle. The owner said both came out of an estate in Georgia. There were also some smaller items as well, which we didn't buy.

The owner's business was hurting as was mine, as this was during the Midwest floods. He said he'd take $40 for the drum and $125 for the altar bottle. I only had about $40 on me, so I grabbed the drum and passed on the altar bottle.

From there on out, items from the occult would find me. I didn't have to look too hard to find such things as antique Ouija boards, scrying mirrors, etc. Most of these items were purchased at rock-bottom prices.

After purchasing the Voodoo drum, we of course were eager to do another channeling session with Haji. During this session, Haji asked where the altar bottle was. When someone told him we couldn't afford it, Haji asked if we would purchase the lantern if we made enough money the following day. We, of course, said yes. The following day we made exactly enough money, within two cents, to purchase the lantern. We made the purchase.

After doing some research, I learned the bottle was from the early 1900s.

A couple of days later Bill suffered a massive stroke, couldn't speak, and was confined to a wheelchair. His lady friend kept the store running for him.

While living in the apartment, strange things started to happen. This was my first experience with a demonic infestation.

CHAPTER 6

THE INFESTED APARTMENT

"The devil loves darkness. He always operates in the dark because he knows that if he is discovered, he is beaten."

Saint John Bosco

The tall, slim, hippy looking guy walked into my store one afternoon. He carried with him a black scrying mirror. On the back of this mirror was a metal pentagram and stained glass. He said he was a witch. He needed gas money in order to return to his home in Oklahoma. He wanted twenty dollars for the mirror. I thought it was a steal at that price.

There was, however, a catch with this item. Only after he took my twenty dollars did he inform me that he believed the mirror was haunted by an impish-looking demon. He told me to cleanse it before any use or ritual work. The mirror was well made and a fine piece of art. After he left, I ritually cleansed the mirror. Within twenty minutes, and right in the middle of the cleansing, the phone rang.

Cathy, at her work in downtown St. Louis, was on the phone. She told me that she believed she had just seen some type of elf-looking entity staring at her through the plants near her. It was very unusual for Cathy to see something like this. Cathy, thinking back to her Catholic faith, was totally unaware that I purchased the mirror and was totally rattled.

I explained the purchase of the mirror to Cathy. I told her that what she was seeing was more than likely the entity from the mirror.

Cathy, although believing in psychics, had her own strong Catholic faith. Although she always trusted me and let me do my own thing, this situation scared the heck out of her. She had never seen an actual manifestation.

I further explained that I was in the process of cleansing the mirror and that the entity probably left the mirror and was attempting to hold on by going to her. After the call, I started over by cleansing the mirror.

Once it was cleansed, I decided to try it out. Using a scrying mirror is pretty easy once you know what you're doing and your eyes have grown accustomed to it. I dimmed the lights, lit a candle, and started to look into the mirror. The first visions I saw were a forest and a stream. Next, looking back at me, was the pointy-eared imp-like entity. Cathy was absolutely right by stating that he looked like an elf, except his face was withered and old.

The face slowly faded. My cleansing hadn't worked. I cleansed the mirror again and retested it. Finally the entity was gone.

Several days later, new neighbors moved into the apartment next door. They came into the store to introduce themselves. Their names were Dwayne and Lisa. Both were in their early twenties. Dwayne was slim with long black hair and Lisa was slightly overweight. Dwayne informed me that they were both Satanists. Shockingly, this didn't really bother me at all. I was so far gone in the evil one's realm that the only religion I didn't like was Christianity. I thought all Christians were hypocrites.

Lisa was an amateur Satanist at best. She couldn't even pronounce Anton LaVey's last name (founder of the Church of Satan) correctly. She kept referring to him as Anton LeeVee. Needless to say, I did develop a short friendship with these people out of pity more than anything else.

Our friendship ended when Lisa hung a Christmas star decoration upside down to form an inverted pentagram in her upstairs window right over the shop. After asking her to remove it, she refused. I tried to explain to her that this may be offensive to my customers who weren't Satanists, as Satanism turned some people off. She still refused.

I let it go. Within a week, they moved out.

Gator and Lydia were staying with us one weekend when the strange events, or should I say preternatural experiences, started to really begin.

For whatever reason, all four of us, when leaving the apartment, would always run down the steps when we were alone. No one ever said anything about this until one day when leaving, Gator fell down the steps. He later claimed he was pushed by some unseen force. Gator told us he was racing down the steps as he usually did, and about the second or third step down he said it felt like two unseen hands violently pushed in the middle of his back. Everyone admitted after Gator said something, that they too, for whatever reason, rushed down the steps as if something were pursuing them.

There were also cold spots in the apartment where the temperature would be ten or twenty degrees colder. These spots were by the fireplace and in the extra bedroom where Gator and Lydia stayed.

I smudged the apartment with a smudge stick in the hopes that whatever it was would leave, but this only ticked it off.

The next strange event occurred when I started to see an apparition out of the corner of my eye. This was an older lady with a Santa Claus apron standing in the corner of the apartment. When I told the others about this, much to my surprise, they admitted seeing the same thing.

The apartment almost always seemed dirty no matter how much it was cleaned. The apartment even in the daytime always appeared dark and dreary.

Then things took on a more ominous tone.

Lydia woke everyone up one night after seeing an apparition of a dark robed figure above her bed. She said that at the same time it appeared, she felt as though she were being strangled.

One evening while cooking dinner, the butcher knife I was using slid off the cutting board on the stove as if being thrown and stuck in the linoleum floor, barely missing my right foot.

Right after the knife incident, all of the knives hanging on the wall with hooks and a magnetic holder came crashing to the ground.

Along with constantly cleansing the apartment, I tried to figure out the source of the activity.

I left a Bible open to Psalm 46; however, this seemed only to stop the activity for a short time, and then it would pick up in a more aggressive manner.

I nailed down the source of the activity to the Satanists next door. I highly doubted they were capable of performing a ritual to summon an entity, but maybe I was mistaken. I considered Bill, but from what I'd heard, he was in no medical shape to do anything. I also thought about the mirror, but after I cleansed it the final time, I sold it, so it was long gone.

The next few nights went without incident.

The following weekend, when Gator and Lydia came up for the weekend, I decided to hold a channeling session with Haji in order to try to find the source of the activity. I also asked him for protection. I knew this may be dangerous with all the other activity going on, but I still had to try.

This went terribly wrong. At first Haji came through as usual. I felt myself slip out of body, which was normal. Then it came. I felt something try to push Haji aside and take over my body; it felt like pure evil. The next thing I knew, Cathy was praying over me, which probably saved my life. Gator and Lydia were holding me down. When they were sure it was me that returned to my body, they gave me the details.

According to Gator, Haji's voice became distant and something else had taken over my body. He said that it sat straight up instead of slightly slouching like Haji did. Gator then said I crossed my legs and took on weird mannerisms. It spoke with hand gestures. It saw one of our cats named Murphy and looked directly at it. It spoke calmly and asked to pet it. Lydia repeatedly asked, "Who are you?" They said it ignored the question. When Cathy picked the cat up, it started stroking it gently, then said something about petting the cat's head. It then looked straight up, clenched its hand around the cat's throat, and said, "I'm going to strangle the little (very vile profanity)!"

Cathy immediately pulled the cat back. Gator and Lydia held me down while Cathy prayed. It then proceeded to speak of evil things. Gator said it told Lydia and him bad things about their pasts that no one knew, then laughed at them.

When I pushed with more questions after I was back in body, no one would talk. Cathy still won't talk about the incident to this day. One thing's for certain, if it weren't for Cathy's Catholic faith, I probably wouldn't be here today.

I was really ticked off that some evil entity had apparently got one over on me. I was taught early on by Bill that a good ritual magician should always remain in control. I was a failure. I felt violated and vulnerable. I once again started to smudge the apartment and perform a banishing ritual.

The only thing I remember was getting a really evil or ominous feeling and something trying to push its way through. Then I remember I just kept floating above my body. I couldn't get back in.

At that time, I in no way thought about how the prayer had worked, nor did I realize at that time that it was the power and faith in Jesus of my friends that saved me. That was the furthest thing from my mind.

I also missed an important event. Cathy's rosary kept getting lost and would then be found in places Cathy never remembered putting it. This particular demon was manipulating religious items. This is a true indicator of demonic infestation being done by a high-ranking demon, as only high-ranking demons are able to manipulate religious objects.

The next night, I started to cleanse the apartment as usual. This was getting to be a daily habit. Gator and Lydia were in the living room watching television, while Cathy was sitting in the other room doing her cross-stitch. As I made my way through the rooms, I stood in the living room looking down the hallway. In the hallway, all lined up, one beside the other, stood our three cats, Mookie, Murphy, and Oreo. They were all watching something in the hallway by our bedroom. I watched as Murphy and Oreo sat up and arched their backs, as cats do when they're being petted. Mookie merely kept hissing at something. As I tried to get everyone's attention, Murphy and Oreo flew backward, as if being thrown or kicked by some unseen force. After landing, Murphy and Oreo joined Mookie in hissing while looking down the hallway. Then they all three stopped at the same time and went their separate ways.

I looked at Gator and Lydia, and they looked at me with wide open mouths. Cathy stood and started praying the Our Father.

The Gator spoke up and said something interesting.

"You cleansed everything, right?" Gator asked.

"Yeah, I said. I left a window open to corner it and chase it out."

"But you haven't cleansed that!" Gator said, pointing to an attic access.

Gator was skinny so he was volunteered to go up into the attic and smudge.

"What the hell!" Gator exclaimed while in the attic.

Gator then started to hand down some of the stuff he found, including old newspapers from the 1960s, as well as old dried-up funeral flowers.

The last item to come down caused us all to look at each other in astonishment. It was a sewing pattern for a kitchen apron with a Santa Claus on front, identically matching the same one worn by the apparition we had all observed.

CHAPTER 7

MEETING HARVEY AND WILLIE'S STUFF

"Padre Pio, you give us more trouble than Saint Michael!"

Voice of a demon when Padre Pio freed the souls of a person possessed by the devil!

The activity in the apartment gradually diminished but never actually stopped. The neighborhood, however, became unsafe. Vietnamese gangs had taken over this area, and they started extorting money from Asian-owned businesses. At night, you could lie in bed and hear gunfire.

Although they never bothered us, the store and the other events were beginning to take a toll on me. When first leasing the store and apartment, I thought it would be great living above the shop. Boy, was I wrong Living above the business definitely had its disadvantages. My customers would ring our doorbell at all hours, even late at night. Their problems were various. As a psychic and root worker, they looked to me for answers.

One client in particular was Ann. Ann never really bothered us; however, one evening around 9 p.m., she rang my doorbell. I left from working on my old McIntosh computer to answer the door.

She was hysterical and crying. She told Cathy and me that her longtime boyfriend had died hours earlier by shooting himself. We both tried to calm her down to no avail. Ann said that she wanted to contact her boyfriend to make sure he was alright on the other side. I told Ann that it was extremely dangerous to do so, as he died a violent death only hours before. I further stated that his soul was probably still in the early stages of transference. This would make it almost impossible to communicate with him.

While talking with Ann, I continued to try working on the computer. All of a sudden, I felt as if I were in a trance. I kept typing the word "kitten" over and over. When I finally forced myself out of the trance, I sat back away from the computer. It still kept typing "kitten" at least four more times on its own. I asked Cathy if the word kitten meant anything to her. Ann interrupted and burst into tears. She said that kitten was her boyfriend's pet name for her. With that remark, I turned off the computer. Ann picked up her coat and left. I never saw her again. Due to the recent demonic infestation in the apartment, I wasn't sure that this was actually from her boyfriend or another entity. As usual with an infestation, there were other spirits present. It was better to be safe than sorry. I smudged the apartment.

Harvey had been a regular customer for quite some time. Harvey was in his mid-forties, about six-foot-two and slightly chunky. He wore glasses and had a gray beard and hair. Harvey was a Satanist with a deep interest in Voodoo. Harvey and I hit it off almost immediately the first time he came in. Although I wasn't a Satanist, I liked Harvey's no-nonsense attitude as well as the fact that he was hysterically funny.

Harvey had been a practicing Satanist for years. He was good friends with Anton LaVey, founder of the Church of Satan, and Peter Gilmore (now head of the Church of Satan), who was Anton's right-hand man. Harvey also has associations with Michael Aquino of the Temple of Set. Needless to say, Harvey ran in some pretty high-ranking satanic circles.

One day, Harvey came in, and I confided in him about the shop, the declining neighborhood, and the endless stream of clients ringing my doorbell. Harvey offered to buy the shop. He said he loved the ambiance of a good declining neighborhood. Although a Satanist, Harvey found humor in nearly everything. After about a week, I contacted Harvey, and the sale was completed. We used part of the money to move into a three-bedroom home further south in the city. Harvey even brought over a bottle of champagne to celebrate. I was really happy for him and the two of us. We have remained friends.

I saw less and less of Gator and Lydia, as I felt they'd seen enough.

I married Cathy in late 1994. Shortly before the wedding, while browsing with Cathy in an antique store one day, I ran across a very strange collection of antique occult items. The collection had come from University City, a suburb of St. Louis. There were old spirit trumpets and old 78 rpm records, with handwritten titles like "The Black Mass" and "Levitation." There was also an old book of rituals, plus a hardcover book entitled *The Planetarian Apocalypse*. There was also an original manuscript to the hardcover book. The author of the book and previous owner of the materials was one William E. Wootten.

Rifling through the ritual book, I kept seeing the name Mephistopheles and the names of several demons that I recognized. Also, there was an original charter certificate for The Church of the Planetarian. The materials were from the late 1940s and went through the 1950s.

There were even old magazines that contained reviews of Mr. Wootten's book. One from a 1957 edition of *Fate* magazine states: "This book describes the 'Revealed Planetary Religion,' definitely a cult with twenty "I believe" clauses."

After thumbing through the book, I discovered it contained information on spells, wraiths, vampires, chaotic monsters, demons, evil fiends, and possession. I went ahead and purchased the lot, despite Cathy's protests. I kept a few things and sold the rest to Harvey.

A few days later, Harvey called me and told me he'd listened to the 78 rpm recordings. He started having nightmares. One recording in particular still gives me chills. These people would chant "Praise to the devil and all of his work" to the Alfred Hitchcock theme.

I thought to myself that, if this stuff scares the heck out of a Satanist, it really must be evil.

Later Harvey researched the group. He paid a visit to the heir of the estate where the lot was purchased. The man who answered the door told Harvey that he wanted nothing to do with Wootten. He did say he was supposed to pick up and lead the cult, as Wootten had no children. With that, he closed the door. Harvey did find out that Mr. Wootten and most of the members of his cult were schoolteachers.

CHAPTER 8

THE PALO FOLLOWERS

"The rosary shall be a powerful armor against hell, it will destroy vice, decrease sin, and defeat heresies."

Saint Francis de Sales

Cathy and I decided to move to Farmington, Missouri. We invested the rest of the proceeds from the sale of the shop into a dollar store. Harvey helped us move. After helping us, I'll never forget Harvey's reaction, "Now how the hell do I get out of Mayberry?" I laughed until I was blue in the face. I continued to keep in contact with Harvey while we lived in Farmington. During every one of our phone conversations, Harvey would ask if I'd had enough of Mayberry and when I was moving back to the city. I continued my practices while living in Farmington. I even found a few like-minded individuals who joined me.

After a few years, in 2005, Cathy and I followed Harvey's advice and moved back to St. Louis. I then opened a second occult/new age store. This store was geared more toward new agers than the past store.

I needed a manager for this store, so I hired a young woman we'll call Susan. Susan was a customer who I thought was into Buddhism. She performed psychic readings at another new age store. She was short and slightly overweight with blondish-red hair. Susan came off as being reputable.

I also got to know her husband David. He was quite large and slightly overweight with glasses.

One day within the first few weeks of opening the store, Susan began telling me about the various groups that would be, more than likely, patronizing my new store.

Susan mentioned a guy named Steve, a friend of David's. She said Steve was the leader of a group called The Order of Satan. She stated this was a dark, high magic group that practiced a wide variety of rituals. One of these rituals Susan referred to as the Great Rite. In this rite, Steve and his girlfriend Jill would perform a sex magic ritual in front of the rest of the group. Susan also said Steve practiced Palo Mayombe and was a Palo priest, or what is commonly referred to as a Palero.

I was unfamiliar with the religion, so Susan explained that it was "unsanctified Santería." Her husband David also practiced Palo. When David had left Steve's group years ago, Steve had been angry.

Palo Mayombe is a religion that originated in the African Congo. Palo is sometimes referred to as African devil worship. It is said to be the world's most powerful form of dark magic. The belief system of Palo was transported to the Caribbean during the slave trade between 1400 AD to 1500 AD and found its way to Cuba and Puerto Rico. The influence of Palo Mayombe can be found in Central and South America, as well as Mexico.

Palo Mayombe, or Palo as it is commonly called by its practitioners, was part of the Santería religion. Devout Santería practitioners normally shy away from Palo, as Palo works with negative and dark energies, whereas they believe Santería works with light and positive energies.

There are many different groups in the Palo religion. Most condone animal sacrifice. Although animal sacrifice is legal in the United States so long as the animal is not treated cruelly or made to suffer needlessly (see the 1993 Supreme Court decision for *Church of Lukumi and Babalú-Ayé, Inc. vs. City of Hialeah*), some Palo practitioners like to step over this line. Some Palo practitioners torture the animals before slaughtering them, because they believe this produces a higher degree of negative energy, which in turn pleases the entity.

Some Palo groups can be linked to drug trafficking and organized crime. One such reference to this is the events that occurred in Matamoros, Mexico, in the 1980s. This particular group practiced human sacrifice. They murdered a young college student from the United States. The group was also heavily involved in the drug trade. (For more on the Matamoros group, see the Chapter 24 section on Palo Mayombe.)

Paleros have even been known to perform spells for such things as keeping the police away, causing mental illness, and death. The spells that keep the police away attract a wide variety of criminal elements.

It wasn't long until Susan said she had contacted Steve, because she was interested in getting initiated into Palo. Steve had lineage (other Palo practitioners who were related to him through initiation) all over the United States and had clients who regularly purchased spell service in several government offices. Thus, Susan started her dark journey into Palo Mayombe.

It was during this time that I also hired a young lady, a friend of Susan's named Mary, to help with year-end inventory.

Mary practiced a religion known as Wicca, which is a pagan, earth-centered religion.

One day, I overheard a conversation between Susan and Mary in which Susan told Mary she was being initiated into Palo. Mary asked Susan if a man named Jim Daniels was still around. I asked Susan who Jim Daniels was. She said, "He's a cop that practices Palo."

Shortly after, I finally met Steve and his girlfriend, Jill. Steve was tall and slim with long scraggly-looking black hair. Jill was an attractive blonde and quite a bit younger than Steve.

Steve and Jill became regular customers of my store. Steve's mother, as well as his stepfather, both in their mid-to-late sixties, also practiced Palo. They too were regular customers.

Steve's Palo sect was named Munanso Rayos, which translated to The House of Rays. The group's primary deity was called Siete Rayos. The deity is the dark equivalent of the Santería deity Chango. Steve supposedly did ritual work for other occult shops in St. Louis.

I blew off most of what Steve and Susan talked about. Although I really didn't approve of their religion, I tried to keep an open mind.

Susan said she had to pay Steve between $2500 to $3000 for her initiation into Palo as a priestess. She said she didn't have all the money, so Steve took payments.

One slow day, Susan asked if I wanted to exchange readings (a common practice among psychics), and I agreed. In doing so, Susan kept trying with emphasis to find out about my personal religious beliefs as well as our financial situation. Little did I know that Susan was going to twist and use the information against me.

CHAPTER 9

THE PALO PRIEST

*"Man commits idolatry whenever he honors and reveres a creature
in place of God, whether this be gods or demons."*

Catechism of the Catholic Church #2113

In 1997, Steve piled into a broken-down Chevy with a friend of
his and headed to South Carolina in search of a becoming an initiate
of a group that practiced Palo. Steve became an initiate of Palo, and
then a Palero. Following initiation, he returned to Missouri.

A regular customer named Molly expressed interest in joining
Steve's Palo sect. Molly had been a regular customer for quite some
time and mostly purchased candles, incense, and crystals. Molly had
apparently been conversing with Susan and Steve. During one of her
visits to the store, I took Molly aside and attempted to explain to
her that, in my opinion, Palo was an evil religion that mostly worked
with negative energies. I said that I didn't feel she should join.

Molly didn't listen and, apparently, told Steve and Susan what
I said, because their attitude toward me changed for the negative.
What compounded this is that I refused their invitation to join
their sect.

People who practice the dark arts have what Harvey and
I referred to as "power trips." These power trips are especially

prevalent when they were working spells, which was almost always. When on these trips, they would become extremely arrogant. Palo practitioners also believe that you can solve almost every problem, even the little ones, with magic. This is definitely not so with the other occult arts. Also, it seemed Steve's sect was constantly involved in some type of magical war or at odds with some other sect. One day, I was talking with Harvey about it. He said that Palo practitioners rarely have any friends or relationships. They usually die alone due to the fact that they always have negative spirits or demons around them. Harvey further reiterated that Palo practitioners think they are in charge of the demons, but in actuality the demons are in charge of them. (This ends up being true in *all* of the occult arts.)

This explained a lot. Especially when they would torture the supposed spirits to make them meaner.

Susan kept pressuring me to find out what I practiced or what my religious beliefs were. Susan knew Cathy was Catholic but wasn't sure exactly what I practiced. I planned on keeping it that way. I figured the less these people knew about me, the better off I was.

One time at the store during Lent, Cathy said she was going to pick up fish at church and asked me and my five-year-old son, Tim if we wanted anything. Susan then made an ignorant comment. She said to my son Tim, "You'd better eat your fish or you'll burn in hell!"

Although I wasn't Catholic at the time, even I was offended by this remark! That same day Susan took a book of mine on Padre Pio that I was reading and picked it up. She took out a prayer card of Padre Pio that I was using as a bookmark. She looked me in the eye and said "One day I'm going to bite you and Padre Pio." "Biting" was Steve's slang term for cursing people.

That did it! I'd had enough. I sat Susan down and told her that my shop was not a recruitment center for Palo and that I found her religious remarks to me offending and harassing. Susan broke down into tears, telling me that Steve was forcing her to pay for her initiation and that he'd curse her if she didn't pay him.

Steve and Jill kept coming into the shop. He never said anything about what I said to Susan, but his attitude toward me was horrific.

I explored several legal remedies to get rid of these people, but none seemed to work without the repercussion of a legal suit being filed by them for religious discrimination.

I just smiled and watched as these people destroyed my business.

Although these people knew a little too much about me, they still couldn't figure out what I practiced. From the research I'd done, I discovered that Palo practitioners don't like Voodoo practitioners, so I told Susan and Steve I was initiated into Voodoo as a priest. Although I studied Voodoo, I was in no way a priest.

Instead of getting rid of them, this only made them angrier. Steve asked by who and where was I initiated. I told him in the Bronx, New York (I knew there were a lot of Voodoo practitioners there). I made up a fictitious name for who initiated me. Steve responded with, "I know him!"

Knowing there's no way he could have known this imaginary person, I now knew what game they were playing.

The next dreadful experience with these people was when Steve came into the store wearing a T-shirt that said vile words about Jesus. Although I didn't consider myself a Christian, I even found it offensive. I told Steve to go home and change, and he left angry.

Steve advertised my store on his website without my permission. Before long, I had tons of Palo and Santería practitioners coming in to see Steve, but they never bought anything.

One Sunday, I decided to pop in unannounced on Susan and Steve just to make sure there were no problems. When I entered the store, I discovered Steve had a young teenage boy behind the counter. I had caught this boy a few days previously trying to steal a book. Susan and Steve knew this young man was barred from the store, but what was even more idiotic was that Steve was apparently tutoring the young man in the black arts. I immediately became enraged and chased the young man off. I then blew up at Steve and Susan for trying to teach or recruit this young man.

Several days passed and Susan and I were sitting behind the counter talking. Susan was discussing with me their sect's latest fight with another sect. She claimed that the sect they were in a fight with had double-crossed them. I bluntly asked Susan what happens to people when they double-cross the sect. She said they either go to jail or attack people and go to a mental institution.

I then asked Susan what the specifications were for entry into their sect. She refused to tell me.

I would find out later that Steve and Susan were using controlling spells against me. This would explain why my ritual work I was doing to get rid of them wasn't working.

As if this weren't enough, my problems with the sect were about to get worse.

CHAPTER 10

THE NGANGA POT

"The whole of man's history has been the story of dour combat with the powers of evil, stretching, so our Lord tells us, from the very dawn of history until the last day."

Catechism of the Catholic Church #409

A few days later, Steve came into the shop and sat down next to me. He apologized for his past behavior. He said he valued my friendship and asked if we could start over.

I agreed to this, but I remained on my guard. I couldn't throw these people out, as they'd sue me on the basis of religious discrimination. I never said anything about what I'd heard about them casting controlling spells against me. I now understand why the spells I was casting to rid myself of them weren't working. Quite simply put, they either had a closer relationship to Satan than I did, or Satan had a tighter hold on them.

I was sort of relieved that Steve had apologized. Even though I didn't approve of their religion, I didn't need all the nonsense.

To show he was sincere with his apology, Steve offered to make me a Lucero at cost. A Lucero in Palo is the equivalent of an Eleguá in Santería. These are little concrete or clay statues that contain magical items connected to the appropriate spirit placed into the statue. In this case, Steve told me he'd make me a Lucero for protection.

I was a little apprehensive about this, but I thought it would be better to accept his gift than to anger him further. Besides, I could get rid of the statue if I felt the need.

One Saturday afternoon, Susan caught three people making occult markings outside of the store. She called me immediately. I suspected this was set up by her and Steve. However, when I got there, there were indeed three people making markings outside the store. I told the three never to come back again. Steve said he recognized one of the three. They were associated with another occult supply store in St. Louis. He said he would take care of the problem because he used to do ritual work for this particular store.

I figured I'd let him handle it. If someone was trying to curse my store, it was better for Steve to handle it than me.

Sunday came and so did a phone call from Steve. Steve asked me to meet him at the shop and said he had the ultimate thing for protection. This made me especially nervous.

A little while later, into the store walks Steve carrying something covered up with a black trash bag. Jill was with him. She was carrying a book.

Steve waited until all of the customers left, then pulled off the trash bag. Underneath was a nganga pot. A nganga pot is a large pot or cauldron that contains a spirit or several spirits; in this case, demons. These pots are considered central to the principal practices of Palo. The pot had several sticks jutting out of it, as well as a ram's skull (real, not a reproduction). There was a large machete in the pot. The pot also had magical symbols painted on the front of it, as well as a padlock and chain around it.

Each of the sticks had a specific purpose and was made of a different imported wood. The ram's skull was real and had come from a previous sacrifice the sect had made. (More on this later.) The purpose of the padlocked chain around the pot was for releasing the demons within. The demons would be released when the padlock was unlocked and bound when it was locked.

Palo practitioners do a lot of research into violent deaths in their area so that they can then add dirt from these areas to the nganga pots. They believe that the spirits of the victims of these violent deaths produce the proper amount of negative energy to work with.

Steve gave me and my mother (she worked in the shop) a supposed prayer to recite, as well as a recipe for making something called chamba. Chamba was a mixture of rum and other herbs. Its purpose was to feed the pot between sacrifices.

Steve said this pot was dedicated to a deity known as Siete Rayos, a Palo deity. This was the main spirit in the pot, besides several other demons.

Supposedly, Palo practitioners torment these demons to make them obey. Every deity in Palo requires a different type of animal to be sacrificed. Chickens were a staple. These animals were purchased from a farmer's market located near downtown St. Louis.

Steve made an altar for the nganga. He placed a drum and a Saint Barbara statue next to the pot. He said offerings, especially apples, were good.

Then Steve showed me a picture of the pot. It was in a book in which someone had written an article about his sect. He said he was showing me the picture to prove this was an actual nganga pot. He further stated that this particular pot was "born" off of his original Palo godfather. To be "born" in Palo means that some of the original dirt from his godfather's pot was placed into this one as a symbol of lineage.

Steve told me that the pot was "off limits" to me and my mother, except to recite the prayers and give offerings. (This was idolatry at its worst!)

The pot really gave me the creeps, but I have to admit I was intrigued, to say the least.

All of the members of the sect—Susan, Steve, Jill, and David—would congregate in my shop. They would talk openly about their sacrifices and exploits.

Steve bragged about how he and David had tortured the very ram whose skull was in the shop's nganga. They said they beat the poor animal all the way home from the market where it was purchased. The ram, so they said, was a special order from the same person that sold them chickens. Steve bragged that the guy selling the animals to them thought Steve was Farmer Brown.

They referred to getting the animals as making a chicken run. Perhaps one of the sickest stories I'd heard was that when no chickens were available and it was time to feed his ngangas, Steve would sacrifice guinea pigs purchased from local pet shops. One day, Steve told how he persistently stabbed the animal. All it did was squeal. Steve said, "It wouldn't (vile profanity) die!"

One day during this period, Steve and I were discussing the events of Matamoros, Mexico, in the 1980s, where a particular Palo sect committed human sacrifices and buried the victims on their ranch. Steve looked at me seriously and said, "Human sacrifices are most pleasing to the deities. They will get you to the top quickly, but you'll soon crash."

Next, Steve said he really needed money, so he offered to sell me the pot. He told me he would help initiate me into Palo. I accepted his offer because I knew that once the pot was technically mine, I could do what I wanted with it. However, I had no desire to be initiated into Palo.

I thought, "Unbelievable!" This guy just talked about murdering people as if they were one of the chickens he regularly sacrificed! I knew right then that this guy was dangerous and could easily hurt someone. I knew I had to get rid of all of them.

My mother and I had been reciting prayers to the nganga, as well as leaving it apples for some time now.

I decided to call someone in Texas to find out more. The person I called was a reputable botanica that had been in business for years. I called and spoke with a man we'll call Enrique. Enrique was an expert in Palo as well as Santería.

I had dealings with Enrique on several occasions when a customer would come into the shop looking for something among the Santería line I didn't have.

I told Enrique about the prayer of protection that Steve had given me and mother to recite to the nganga. Enrique told me that this was not a protection prayer. Instead, its purpose was to bind you to the pot as well as Siete Rayos.

Enrique said it was a good thing that I owned the pot as I could "clean" the spirit and disassemble the pot and destroy it. Enrique told me to go to a Catholic church and acquire a bottle of holy water, which I did. He then told me to pour it into the dirt in the pot. Enrique said to call him back if I noticed anything strange.

Within thirty minutes, Steve called and said something was going on. He had to change or switch one of the rocks in the pot, and so he needed the pot back. I told him no, because the pot was mine and to leave it alone for a while. This wasn't out of the ordinary, so I didn't call Enrique.

About forty-five minutes after that, Steve called back and asked if I knew of anyone that could be messing with the pot. Now this was strange! I answered no and called Enrique.

Enrique said that the spirits were turning on Steve. He thought that I should now destroy the pot. He gave me in-depth instructions for disassembling it.

I, however, had other ideas. I thought if holy water worked, then a cross would really work. I looked around the shop and found a small wooden cross. I soaked it in holy water, then placed it beneath the dirt in the pot.

Later that night Steve's girlfriend, Jill, was in an almost fatal auto accident that totaled their car.

I was on a magical power trip just like them. I wasn't done yet. I continued with the same actions for a little less than a week.

Some other things happened. Steve and Jill's pets got sick, and they claimed some other sect was trying to curse them.

Finally, Steve came into the shop and insisted that someone was messing with the pot. On a magical power trip, I answered, "Of course!" Dark magic can be like a drug. Practitioners get a little power behind them by means of performing a ritual, and so it gets addictive.

Although I didn't realize it at the time, I was slowly coming under the influence of the demons in the pot.

CHAPTER 11

DUMPING THE NGANGA POT

"All practices of magic or sorcery, by which one attempts to tame occult powers ... are gravely contrary to the virtue of religion. These practices are even more to be condemned when accompanied by the intention of harming someone, or when they have recourse to the intervention of demons."

Catechism of the Catholic Church #2117

Susan returned from vacation in a most unusual way. She came into the shop carrying her Lucero in a wicker basket that was covered in fresh chicken blood. I told her to get out and take her basket with her. Instead, she said, "You'll have to throw me out." She then sat in a chair and began rocking back and forth while chanting something in either Spanish or an African language. When she was finished, she picked up her Lucero and left. I told her not to return for three days. This ticked her off.

Molly, whom I strongly suspected had joined Steve's sect, came into the shop the day after Susan's escapade. She asked if she could speak with me in private. Molly claimed that during her Palo initiation ceremony that happened at Susan's apartment, she was asked to strip naked. Steve anointed her vulva with oil. Following this ritual, Steve claimed they'd spent money to cleanse her, so Molly should be obligated to them.

Molly said her hair was falling out and that she felt nauseous after the ritual.

She asked me if I could cleanse her to be free of the negativity. I gave her some free supplies for the purpose and apologized to her. I told her to go home and take a cleansing bath. She also asked if I would pray with her at a Catholic church, so I accompanied her. Her previous religion was Catholic. I was cautious with Molly because I highly suspected Steve's sect was setting me up.

I now had a complaint from a customer, even if Molly was from Steve's sect. This gave me sufficient grounds to get rid of all of them and stop them from coming into the shop. That's exactly what I did.

Later that evening, I received a phone call from Steve. He was furious that Susan had been fired. Her firing meant that he couldn't collect his initiation money from her. He and Jill were still without a vehicle since the accident. He asked me if I would consider hiring Jill to work in the shop. Although I didn't and wouldn't, I fed him full of disinformation. I told him I would consider it so long as Susan and David had nothing to do with it. I said that he and Jill would have to lay low for a while and stay away until things calmed down after the incident with Molly.

The sect was nervous, very nervous, not because of Molly, as she was one of them, but because their precious pot of demons was in my possession. They no longer had contact with me or the shop, and I was in total control of the pot.

Helena was another customer who fell between the cracks right into Steve's sect. She was a regular customer whose Hispanic heritage demanded something more. Steve was right there to offer it.

She, of course, knew about the pot that I had purchased. Helena had a pretty famous mother who was a psychic in Mexico. Helena told Cathy and me that she had spoken with her mother in Mexico, who thought I should get rid of the pot. She said that one Sunday when Steve was in the shop, he was telling customers that he was controlling me with the pot.

My response was a sarcastic, "I'm sure he was, but not now!"

I argued with Helena over the pot's disposal, as I wanted to keep it. If nothing else, I wanted it for added security against the sect.

I knew that Steve was behind sending Helena there to dispose of the pot. My wife, however, had a different idea! Her Catholic upbringing was telling her the pot was evil and so she wanted it *gone*!

So Helena, Cathy, and I disposed of the pot using Helen's mother's instructions, which from what Enrique told me were accurate.

When we got to the center of the pot, the smell of death was intense. This was mixed with the putrid smell of fragrant oils and cheap perfumes that Steve had used for spell casting.

I did, however, notice something peculiar. Enrique gave me instructions to open the padlock so I used an old lockpick set I had. This would release the spirit back on Steve. Helena didn't unlock the padlock. This totally destroyed the demons inside, or so it was supposed to. That way they couldn't be used again.

The smell of death came from several scorpions that Steve had buried alive in the center of the pot. Later, I found that the use of scorpions in Palo causes mental disorders, as well as intense possession by demons.

Helena also disposed of the Lucero, but she didn't break it open, because this would release the spirit or spirits inside. She threw it away whole—another thing Enrique had told me that caught my attention.

Helena disposed of the last of the pot's contents, the drum, and the Lucero into a garbage bag and then threw it into the back dumpster.

The sect had forgotten one thing by sending Helena in to destroy the pot. The pot was *mine*, not *theirs*! They, in addition, never counted on what I did next.

I was certain that the Lucero was the item that was being used to try to control me with Steve's spells.

Shortly after Helena left, for whatever reason, perhaps under the influence of the demons in the pot, I went outside and climbed into the dumpster and retrieved the pot's inner contents, the drum, and the Lucero. The pot's contents consisted of a brass key, some coins, and a few other objects, and, oh yes, a human neck bone. Steve claimed to purchase these bones from an internet site; however, Palo practitioners have been known to actively participate in grave robbing.

This particular bone was believed by the sect to hold all of the body's stresses. They referred to it as the atlas bone.

These bones, as well as the graveyard dirt placed into the pot, are believed to contain the spirits of the deceased. Paleros sometimes seek those who have died under violent circumstances as they believe this dirt contains a lot of negative energy.

I placed the drum that Steve had previously placed next to the pot into a display case. Intentionally, I put a high price on the drum. I wanted to send a message to them that the pot's contents were still in my possession.

I knew I couldn't call Enrique back because he'd simply tell me to leave it alone and probably to pour holy water all over it.

I wanted to reconstruct the pot. Perhaps the demons were telling me to do it. So I called another botanica in Hialeah, Florida. They, in turn, referred me to a man named Alberto in Orlando, Florida. Alberto was a Cuban immigrant in his fifties who had practiced Palo nearly all his life.

I received Alberto's complete life story when I called. He was extremely nice. Alberto gave me complete instructions on what to do with the old contents in order to reconstruct the pot. He also told me how to turn the Lucero's contents into an Eleguá, or Santería protective deity statue. I purchased several items from him that were needed in addition to what I already had.

When the rest of the items arrived by FedEx, I took everything home and started the rituals and assembly of the new pot and Eleguá. Bringing the items into my home was a big mistake. From the time Steve had placed the pot in the store, it was never moved until Helena moved it. Now I had moved these items into my home.

A few days later, Steve called and asked if he could meet with me about his girlfriend, Jill, coming back to work. I agreed, as I couldn't wait for him to see the drum.

Steve's parents, also Palo practitioners, arrived before Steve. Steve's mother played along and asked me what happened to the pot. I told her the truth. I said it was at home. She then pinched me on the cheek and said, "Just so Siete is OK!"

"What a crock!" I thought. This old lady surely deserved an Academy Award for the great act she was putting on.

I said I was getting thirsty and wanted to step out for a water. Steve's stepdad offered to get me some water and left. A few minutes later, the stepdad came in with a case of Dasani water. I thanked him, but there was no way in hell I was going to drink that stuff, because it was probably cursed. I told him I got a drink from the bathroom sink while he was gone because I couldn't wait.

Steve and Jill arrived. Steve looked at the display case with the drum in it. They didn't say a word. In fact, nobody said a word.

Steve said he was finished with Susan and David. Of course, I didn't believe anything he had to say. I kept Steve on the hook by telling him that I still couldn't hire his girlfriend, as I had spoken with Molly. She was still thinking of filing charges against them.

Steve also said that Susan was going to sue me for wrongful termination. I told Steve to tell her to expect a countersuit.

As they all got ready to leave, I followed them out the door with Steve right in front of me. As the parents got into their car, Steve and Jill stopped for some last words. They continued to talk about Susan and David in a derogatory manner. Steve then said, "I could just kill those two!"

"I feel the same way," I added.

Steve said, "You know, I could do away with them using the spirits; after all, I'm a Palero!"

I shrugged and opened the door to reenter the store and said, "Whatever!"

I knew something was up and where this was probably going, but I decided to play along anyway.

CHAPTER 12

THE PALO COP

"Satan or the devil and the other demons are fallen angels who have freely refused to serve God and his plan.... They try to associate man in their revolt against God."

Catechism of the Catholic Church #414

As I was opening the store one morning, I noticed Helena pulling into the parking lot. She came into the store and handed Cathy and me a package of Mexican coffee. She told us that her mother had sent her too much and so she was giving some to us. I accepted the gift, and after she left, it went immediately into the trash. There was no way I, nor anyone else in my family, was going to drink that garbage because it was probably cursed.

This was the last time I ever saw Helena. Now that the drum was visible in the case and the sect knew about it, they were still unsure about what Helena did with the pot. They probably were angry with her and sent her packing.

Steve contacted me several days later. He told me that after careful divination, the spirits wouldn't let him kill Susan and David using magic. He said he found someone to "do the job." Knowing that I was probably being taped, but still wanting to play along to see where this would go, I responded as before with a "whatever."

Now I knew I was about to be set up in some sort of murder for hire scheme.

I ignored Steve's calls for about a week, hoping he'd just go away until one day he walked into the store with another man. Steve asked to speak with me in private, so we went to the back while the other man remained in the front of the store.

Steve uttered a slew of vulgarities loud enough for the other customers in the store to hear. I got really close to him and pointed my finger at his chest. I told him to be quiet. He then demanded that I pay him five thousand dollars to have Susan and David murdered.

I got even closer than before. I told him he was an idiot for even insinuating that. I said to take his supposed hit man and get out. He complied, and they both left.

Not smart enough to grasp my message, Steve called once again. This time, he said his supposed hit man was really ticked off that he didn't get his money. He still demanded the five thousand dollars.

At this point, I was boiling mad at the idiot's persistence to contact me after being told not to. I decided to get even with Steve and his sect, as well as put all of the idiots into one basket. Perhaps it was the influence of Siete Rayos, perhaps pure anger, I don't know.

I cut him off. Knowing I was probably being taped, I said, "If I really wanted to kill Susan, all I'd have to do is call K——. But I'm not going to do that. I don't need your help or your hit man, so leave me alone!" I hung up.

By recording me in the state of Missouri and using the tape for his exploits, Steve was committing wiretapping.

I finally thought I was rid of Steve and all the problems.

About two days later, in March 2006, two men entered my store. One was dressed in camouflage pants and a ball cap. He was slim. The other man was older, chubby, and dressed in slacks and a blue windbreaker.

The man in camouflage pants showed me a badge from a necklace hanging on his neck. He identified himself as Sergeant Jim Daniels of the local police department; *the same Daniels who my former employee Susan had to referred to as "a cop that practices Palo!"* I assumed what Susan said in front of Mary earlier about this cop was true.

The other man wouldn't identify himself. I knew right then and there, as I used to be a reserve cop, something was terribly wrong.

The two men escorted me down to the police satellite station three doors down from my store. Jim Daniels did most of the talking. He interrogated me about the comments I made to Steve earlier on the phone. He said I was involved in a murder for hire scheme.

Sergeant Daniels said the supposed hit man Steve was talking about had turned Steve and me in and recorded Steve's conversation. He added that this hit man didn't want to go back to prison.

During the stupidest line of questioning I'd ever heard, Sergeant Daniels seemed to be preoccupied, not with murder for hire, but where the nganga pot was and what happened to it.

I told him that it was at my home and he could come see it if he wanted. He refused. I did tell him I replaced the human bone, just for kicks, and that I had turned over the old bone to a cop who was a friend of mine. He demanded to know who, but I wouldn't tell. The only thing that I told Daniels that wasn't true was that I had been feeding Steve and his "blood cult" full of disinformation.

The chubby older man then spoke. He started to make derogatory comments about my store. I told him that he was making jokes about my religious beliefs.

These two were, much like Steve, complete idiots!

The two then escorted me back to the store. They asked if I would show them Steve's website on my computer. I agreed, and while standing there, they noticed a book about Padre Pio that was sitting on the desk. Sergeant Daniels started talking about Padre Pio. He told my wife he was Catholic, which was a blatant lie.

I noticed Daniels had started looking at the drum in the case. When he'd catch me looking at him, he'd quickly look at something else. So me and my big mouth decided to ask him, "Do you like my drum, Sergeant?"

He refused to answer and gave me a dirty look. I requested his phone number.

My mother then spoke up and asked if animal sacrifice was legal. He said, "Yes, it is!" With that, he and his anonymous cohort left.

As I thought about different things that Steve's sect had done, and tripping on black magic, I would call Daniels. He'd just hang up. One time he told me he was in the middle of a dope deal. What an idiot!

Even after all of this, the next day Steve's mother and stepfather were parked in front of the store, waiting for it to open. I went to a convenience store pay phone down the street to call Daniels.

I told him that I knew he practiced Palo and that I wanted these people removed from my store. He reluctantly did so.

The following day when I received a call from Steve, I immediately called the police. This still didn't work, as little did I know, Steve wasn't finished with me yet.

I have the utmost respect for cops and law enforcement because I used to be a security officer, but this guy was up to no good. Not to mention that since he practiced Palo, he was protecting Steve's sect, which was torturing and killing animals.

When you cast a curse, intimidation, such as what Steve and Daniels were doing to me, plays a big factor. I got the feeling something like a curse was about to follow.

CHAPTER 13

THE BEGINNING OF THE CURSE AND POSSESSION

"Remember that the devil doesn't sleep but seeks our ruin in a thousand ways."

Saint Angela Merici

Molly reentered the store one day accompanied by her friend, Missy. Of course, I knew these two were up to no good, but I had to serve them. Molly said she was interested in purchasing an Eleguá. She also asked me a lot of questions concerning the religion of Santería.

The only Eleguás I had were hollow, which meant they weren't completely finished. It was up to the customer to ritually prepare and finish them. I told Molly she'd have to complete the Eleguá herself.

In Santería, Eleguá is known as a trickster spirit.

Molly and Missy both had a couple of macutos, which are cowry shells wrapped in beads geared toward the colors of a particular deity. In their case, these belonged to Chango, the Santería equivalent of Siete Rayos. Molly and Missy began kissing the macutos and saying praises to Chango. This was similar to Susan's little act with the Lucero covered in chicken blood.

Molly then said Steve was casting a curse on me. He was using an audiotape he had recorded of me. I asked her if it was the same one that involved the hit man. She shut her mouth. After they left, Molly would stoop to making childish prank phone calls to the store asking for information about Voodoo, but then bad mouthing it. The last phone call I received from Molly was about the information on Voodoo.

One evening while at home outside on our deck, I began to feel nauseous and thought I may be coming down with something. This was accompanied with severe chills and a tingling feeling on the back of my neck. This was the same tingling feeling I received when a spirit was about to enter my body. I felt as though there was a heavy waterfall on top of my head, pressing down.

Moments later I heard, "Daddy, Daddy!" It was my six-year-old son Tim screaming for help. I immediately went inside to see what was wrong. I rushed into the dining room to find him hiding underneath the table. When I asked what was wrong, he said, "There's someone in my room!" Though thinking this was just a child's roaming imagination, I went down the hall to investigate. I arrived just in time to see a big, black, shadowlike mass hovering above the ground. The mass then appeared to travel through the wall and disappear.

I recognized this as a possible demonic presence. I smudged the house, opened the Bible, and repeated Psalm 46.

I told my wife and mother (who now lived with us) what was going on.

Later that night, the nauseous feeling worsened, and I became extremely depressed. I even had crying spells for no particular reason. The only explanation I can give is that it was like there was an overwhelming amount of negativity and sadness hanging over me. My son even brought me one of his stuffed animals and said,

"He will make you feel better!" Knowing how this was affecting my family made me even more depressed.

I finally contacted some religious friends of mine, named Lynn and George, who came over. In between sobs, I told them the whole story. They advised me to get rid of the nganga pot and its remnants, which they did. Lynn, a devout Catholic, anointed my head with a special oil that was given to her from Father Peter Mary Rookey. This was my first encounter with Father Rookey, although my wife had seen him at a prayer service when we lived in Farmington. Father Rookey, a truly remarkable man, was a healing priest who resided in Chicago.

This anointing calmed me and put me at peace for the night. Although I slept lightly, I did get a little sleep.

The next day I tried to get some more sleep but couldn't.

The crying spells continued as did the feelings of depression and anxiety. Lynn had left some of the oil, but it wasn't working to the extent it had earlier.

The following day, I was still awake. I thought I was going crazy. I had been thinking of Steve and his sect constantly. Everything was running through my head at lightning speed. I thought of Sergeant Daniels and what we said to each other. I thought of Susan when she was rocking back and forth with her chicken blood-covered statue. I thought of evil things I wanted to do to Steve and Daniels. I thought of evil things that Steve and Daniels wanted to do to me. The whole thing was a whirlwind of fear, paranoia, anxiety, and depression that hit me like a freight train.

In the past, I'd never encountered such a thing. I'd stood on strike lines toe to toe with angry teamsters but was never more afraid than this.

The most frightening thing was the shadow my son and I had seen. Would it attack my family? What was its next move?

I told my wife I needed to go to the hospital. I was a wreck. The sleep deprivation was really beginning to take its toll on me. When I arrived at the hospital, I didn't even know what day it was when the doctor asked me. I was that tired and out of it.

I even took copies of Steve's website with me because I wanted the people at the hospital to believe what I was involved in.

A security guard stayed with me and prayed with me. During his prayers, I began to slap him, not out of anger, but because I felt like I needed to. It was as if something was making me do it. They gave me some type of medication that knocked me out. Before I went completely out, Cathy said I asked for apples, the same offering we had made to Siete Rayos.

When I got to my hospital room, I slept the rest of the day and well into the next. My mind finally began to function properly with the right amount of rest. I wasn't certain whether I was under the control of a demon or if it was my imagination. Either way, I needed to figure it out and be rid of it quickly.

CHAPTER 14

OUR LADY OF LOURDES INTERCEDES

"O Holy Spirit, descend plentifully into my heart.
Enlighten the dark corners of this neglected dwelling
and scatter there thy cheerful beams."

Saint Augustine

I was discharged from the hospital a couple of days later. The doctor's diagnosis was that I'd had a nervous breakdown. He sent me home with some mild tranquilizers.

Two days later, I started experiencing severe abdominal cramping. I naturally thought that it was due to the medication I was taking; however, my mother experienced the same symptoms. This led me to believe it might be food poisoning.

My cramping eventually stopped, but my mother's didn't. After ruling food poisoning out, I thought there may be a chance this was some sort of an illness caused by Steve. After all, my mother was the only other family member working in the store. What further heightened my suspicions is that the bowels, the dirtiest part of the body, are usually the first thing infected by some sort of curse. Almost all occultists know this.

I asked my mother if she'd had any contact with anything Steve may have had. She went to her purse and pulled out a small vial. She said Steve's stepfather brought it to her after she had discussed her heart problems with him. After reading the label, I discovered that this was some type of herbal concoction that was supposed to help the heart. It was purchased at a local herb store, but what worried me was the fact that it was probably cursed. Although I never expressed my concerns to her, I took the vial away and told her that she would have to quit taking it. It was also during this time that the feelings of depression and anxiety started again, although they weren't as severe.

Then the nightmares started. The first nightmare was that two entities were watching me sleep. They were humanlike, except their faces were black and broken, and they had glowing white eyes. They merely watched at the foot of my bed. When I'd wake up, it felt as though my mattress was breathing on its own.

Next, a fair amount of preternatural activity occurred in our home. A closet door would open itself all the time when I was in the basement using the computer.

After some nightmares, the TV would come on, or if it was already on, the volume would go all the way up.

Lights would go off in the basement, leaving me in pitch darkness.

One night, I had a horrible nightmare about Siete Rayos in the form of a ram with human features butchering young children.

This is also when I started to see the apparition of a young boy in suspenders and knickers. He wore a white button-down shirt.

At first, I only saw him out of the corner of my eye in the basement. I then had a disturbing dream about him. I was in the bathroom looking in the mirror. As I turned to leave, I almost ran right into him. He turned without saying anything, exited the bedroom, and went down the hall. His face looked normal, except for one eye that looked like he'd been in some sort of an accident and lost the eye. This told me the apparition may have been demonic in nature, as most demonic apparitions appear with something wrong with them, such as a leg missing, eye missing, etc.

My suspicions were confirmed when he motioned for me to follow him. I did. He led me to a closet that contained many firearms. This apparition then put his finger to his head, making the motion of a gun with his pointer and thumb. Then he moved the thumb as if he were shooting himself in the head. My first thought was that he was telling me he had been shot in the eye. In attempting to communicate with him (something you should *never* do), I pointed to his eye. He then shook his head and pointed back at me, stuck his tongue out, and laughed, although he made no sound.

After the dream, I felt very depressed and anxious.

This is when the strange urges started. Much like the feelings I had with obsessive-compulsive disorder and counting things, except a little different and a lot stronger. I would feel compelled to move the TV to the floor for no reason, throw a soda can across the room, etc. These urges were in no way caused by anger, but more like impulsiveness that I couldn't control.

Then these urges took a turn for the worse. I had urges to attack people, or impulses as I should say, as these never involved anger. These urges started gearing themselves toward my wife. Later I would rationalize that this would always occur at the same time of the year, February to March. I would also figure out that my wife was targeted, due to her devout Catholic beliefs. Whether or not Steve was controlling this, I am unsure.

For no reason whatsoever, I would slap at her, much as I slapped at the security guard at the hospital. This slapping wasn't hard, but easy. I would also know when she was praying. This would start the impulsive urge to slap her.

While riding in the car, I would have the impulse to grab the steering wheel. I would try to fight it off, to no avail.

The abdominal cramps also came back as well. The doctors could find nothing wrong.

I faintly remembered what Susan had said about what happens to people if they crossed Steve's sect. She said you go to jail or you attack people. This was exactly what I was doing. I was attacking people.

I was totally coming apart. I knew something had to be done. I also knew, from my experience in the occult, that I was slowly becoming totally possessed by whatever was forcing me to do these things.

I remembered how Paleros can cause mental illness or make mental illness worse.

I called my Palo expert in Orlando. I told him what was going on. He told me how to perform a cleansing ritual on myself; however, I was in no shape to do it. He said I was under a strong spell and that he couldn't break it. He said I had to do it. I was at the end of my rope!

While I was sick and my mother was working in the store, another one of Steve's cronies stopped in. This was an older Hispanic woman with dark hair. She was probably in her sixties.

This woman gave my mother a baby Jesus statue with a tear running down his cheek. The woman claimed the statue was from Mexico. My mother brought the statue home. I wanted to destroy it, but she argued with me. So I let it go.

One day, I couldn't control the overwhelming urge to slap at Cathy. I knew she was praying to herself, so I went up and started to slap her. She immediately called an ambulance, and I was transported back to the hospital.

During this whole encounter, I knew I was becoming fully possessed by something as I wasn't angry and couldn't control my actions. I thought about the Lucero, a trickster spirit. Could it have been that the Lucero was the whole key to this?

The nightmares continued to get worse. I also had suicidal tendencies. The medications the doctor prescribed weren't working.

When I arrived home, my wife was distant. She couldn't tolerate it anymore. We came close to our marriage ending in divorce. This causing of marital strife is another trait of the demonic, as it likes to cause chaos and proceeds to tear families apart.

Cathy told me that someone from the local parish was going to Lourdes, France. They asked anyone who wanted their petitions carried there to write them and bring them to the parish office. I thought, "Why not?" After all, I was at the end of my rope. I wrote out something along the lines of "Blessed Mother, please heal me of this demonic influence. Please get rid of it." I signed my name, placed it into an envelope, and took it to the parish office.

A week later, I had a wonderful dream of the Blessed Mother looking down on me and smiling. When I awoke, I thought I smelled flowers, although there weren't any flowers around. I woke up feeling better than ever. I later discovered that my petition was at Lourdes the day before this occurred.

Around this time, my mother and Lynn were going to Chicago to visit Father Rookey. Father Rookey recommended that I say the Chaplet of Saint Michael. Upon their return, I purchased one and started saying it. I also said the Prayer to Saint Michael. What was really strange was that the more I prayed, the better I felt. I then started saying the rosary. Between these two items and the special anointing oil I was using, as well as Father Rookey's and everyone's prayers, I began to feel better.

I owe my life to the parish member going to Lourdes, Our Lady of Lourdes, Father Rookey, and everyone else who was praying for me. Although the scars of this will remain with me and my family forever, I slowly started healing and I still continue to heal every day.

This was very strange, as the medication I was taking wasn't working, but prayer was!

Around this time my mother, Cathy, and I had a long conversation about the shop. The lease was coming up for renewal, but I no longer wanted any part of it. I wanted to stop my occult practices altogether. We all decided to close the business. My mother and I talked about entering the next Rite of Christian Initiation of Adults class together in order to become Catholics.

For those of you who are unaware of Father Rookey, let me explain. Father Rookey was a Servite priest who had the ability of allowing God to work through him to heal. If you asked him to heal something, he'd simply respond with a smile and say, "I don't heal, God does the healing. He merely uses me."

Father Rookey is one of the most remarkable people I've ever met. Though in his nineties, Father Rookey still continued to say mass every day and still ran his ministry, International Compassion Ministries. He's a very loving and caring man.

I thought my encounter with the demonic was finally over, but little did I know the devil wasn't finished with me yet.

CHAPTER 15

THE DEVIL'S LAST STAND

"Do you want to outwit the devil?
Never let him catch you idle. Work, study, pray,
and you will surely overcome your spiritual enemy."

Saint John Bosco

The preternatural activity in my home gradually diminished until it was all gone.

The devil, however, had something else in mind, and so he came back and gave me a reminder of what I'd endured.

One day I was looking at my credit card statement. I noticed there was an unauthorized charge for a botanica located in Texas. I contacted the charge card company to dispute the debt. They told me this place was classified as a religious supply store.

I then remembered one evening I had left my wallet in the store. I had called Susan to retrieve it for me.

I was suspicious of how this charge happened. I called the number on the statement, but they could only speak Spanish. Needless to say, my Spanish was very broken.

I finally looked this place up on the internet. I discovered it was a store that sold Palo Mayombe supplies. I called Enrique in Texas, who told me that he had never had any dealing with that company. He said he would try to call it to see who charged something and where it was shipped.

Enrique called back and told me that the lady was rude and hung up on him when he talked about a stolen card number. I thought about turning it over to the police, but I didn't know who had used it. I thought they'd never bother to trace it because the charge was for only a hundred or so bucks. Susan must have gone through my wallet and written down the number. She probably gave it to Steve. I knew from talking with Susan that Steve's Palo lineage went to Texas.

This triggered my last bout with Satan. As before, I felt there was a struggle of good versus evil going on inside of me. I thought I would be framed by Steve in some sort of conspiracy. He could easily have planted items purchased with my credit card at some type of crime scene. I started destroying religious items.

Then I stopped and thought, "What if I pray about the situation and ask Jesus, the Blessed Mother, and Saint Michael for help?" That's exactly what I did. The fear and anger of what I was dealing with went away.

My mother's abdominal cramps still continued. She eventually went to see the doctor. They discovered she had lung cancer. Without chemotherapy, they gave her about two months to live. With chemo, she would have a little longer.

My mother's first move, after making appointments for chemotherapy, was to call Father Rookey. Father Rookey prayed with her, as well as sent her a prayer cloth and some more oil especially meant for cancer patients. The oil was called Saint Peregrine oil. It was named after the patron saint of cancer patients. Both of these items, as well as her rosary, were blessed by Father Rookey.

The doctors agreed that her abdominal cramps were caused by the spreading of the lung cancer.

During one of her conversations with Father Rookey, he told her that her cancer would be cured.

About a month and a half later, something remarkable happened. My mother was hospitalized with the abdominal cramps. The oncologist stopped by. He said that the cancer was in remission and almost gone. Although she was getting chemo, I firmly believe it was with Father Rookey's help and prayers that the Lord cured my mother of cancer.

However, we finally discovered that the abdominal cramps were being caused by a bowel obstruction that the doctors had missed. Her bowel was dying, and there was nothing they could do.

My mother's last wish was to become Catholic. I went to my local parish and asked the priest if there was any way he could do something to fulfill this wish. He visited her shortly afterward in the hospital, and, after some prayers, she was Catholic.

Mom kept either her rosary or the prayer cloth in hand at all times. She was very excited about this. She excitedly told everyone who entered her room to see her that she was Catholic.

My mother went home to heaven on a chilly October evening.

I was really ticked off at her death. For whatever reason, I had the urge to destroy religious items again. I stopped. I realized this was a trick of the devil, so I prayed about the matter.

About an hour later, I thought about the baby Jesus statue that was given to Mom by the lady from Mexico. I knew she was a member of Steve's sect because she had asked the price of the drum in the cabinet. Before she left the shop, she and I had exchanged words.

I located the statue and did something that should have been done a long time ago. I smashed the statue to pieces. Palo sects have been known to curse or bastardize Christian religious items then pass them on to unsuspecting victims. I did feel funny smashing a statue of Jesus, but I reconsidered when I thought about how Steve's sect had bastardized the image of our Lord. After the statue was gone, it felt like a ton of weight was lifted off my shoulders.

I still continued to pray every day, and I started going to deliverance ministry. After each deliverance session, I would feel more at peace.

CHAPTER 16

FORGIVENESS

"Bless those who persecute you; bless and do not curse. Rejoice with those who rejoice, and weep with those who weep. Be of the same mind toward one another; and do not be haughty in mind, but associate with the lowly. Do not be wise in your own estimation. Never pay back evil for evil to anyone. Respect what is right in the sight of all men. If possible, so far as it depends on you, be at peace with all men. Never take your own revenge, beloved, but leave room for the wrath of God, for it is written, 'Vengeance is mine, I will repay,' says the Lord. 'But if your enemy is hungry, feed him, and if he is thirsty, give him a drink; for in so doing you will heap burning coals on his head.' Do not be overcome by evil, but overcome evil with good."

Romans 12:14–21

After my mother's death, I still continued to pray and continued to feel better. I did, however, have a lot of anger directed at Steve and his sect because I felt they contributed largely to my mother's death.

Shortly before my mother's funeral, I called Father Rookey's office and requested some materials on how people could contribute to his ministry in memory of my mother. He comforted me with a blessing. It was then that I realized it was nearly over.

I truly believed that our Lord, Saint Michael, and the Blessed Mother had healed me and are still continuing to do so.

I sold Harvey most of the inventory that was left at my shop. Not too long after my mother's death, Harvey contacted me. He was worried that one of the items I had sold him had been cursed by Steve's sect prior to my selling it to Harvey. I admitted it was definitely possible because Susan and Steve had access to the whole store while my mother and I weren't there.

Harvey loves cats. He had a bunch of kittens that he took to his shop. One day a customer was in his store and went to pick up a kitten. The woman screamed because, instead of being asleep, the kitten was dead. Harvey also said he had the worst luck. He felt as though he was cursed. The death of his pet only further confirmed his suspicions. He said he was going to cleanse the item with a cleansing ritual. I told him to let me know how it went.

In the meantime, I entered the RCIA program at my local church. During one part of the RCIA instruction, each of the participants in the program met with parish head, Monsignor Weber.

I spoke with the monsignor at great length about Steve and his sect and expressed my anger toward them. I never will forget what the monsignor told me. He told me not to punish them. Put the matter into God's hands, and he'll judge them. He added that if Steve and his sect were doing the things that I said they were doing, it would eventually catch up with them.

After I thought about the monsignor's words carefully, everything made sense. I would simply drop the anger, as it was another one of Satan's tactics. I put the matter into God's hands.

A few days later, Harvey called me back and said he'd ran into Steve and Jill at a store close to downtown. He said Steve was bragging about killing my mother. Harvey said they were on their way to the farmers market for a chicken run.

Harvey asked, "What do you want to do about this idiot? You and I could curse the hell out of him."

I thought for a little while and pondered the monsignor's words. I couldn't help but think of a WWJD bracelet that my wife had given my son to wear. So I asked myself, "What would Jesus do?"

I was no longer an occult practitioner; I was now a Christian.

It didn't take long before I had the answer. I felt the power to forgive. I realized that what Steve was saying were merely Satan's words.

After all that I'd been through, I finally realized that Jesus's and Mary's power *cannot* be obstructed by Satan. Although he may try, they will always prevail. I also thought that with one's own free will, one either serves Satan or the Lord. I chose serving the Lord.

I told Harvey, "Just tell him next time you see him that I forgive him!"

With that remark, I knew it was finally over, or at least nearly over. Harvey then asked me to call him if I changed my mind. With that, we ended our conversation. After hanging up, I felt an overwhelming sense of peace and relief.

My final dealing with Steve wasn't really a contact, but it shocked the heck out of me. On a warm day, almost three years exactly to the day of my breakdown right after Sergeant Jim Daniels's visit, I was watching the evening news while eating a quick supper before my son's baseball practice. I saw a picture of Steve on the TV. Monsignor Weber was exactly right, as Steve's demons apparently had caught up with him. He went completely crazy and shot his former girlfriend's boyfriend two times, and then held his parents, his girlfriend, and her injured boyfriend hostage for about two hours in a police standoff. The reporter finished by saying Steve was being held on $250,000 bond. Steve is now serving a long prison sentence.

A few years later, Sergeant Daniels's demons caught up with him as well. He eventually had a severe nervous breakdown and was removed from the force.

The Aftermath

As I pondered the monsignor's words after hearing about Steve, I actually felt sorry for him. I felt sorry for Steve because he was so into Satan (or Satan was into him) that he probably will never feel the love of Jesus, but I still pray that there's hope.

Following my years of occult practices, I started attending mass on a regular basis. I continue to say the rosary, chaplet of Divine Mercy, Chaplet of Saint Michael, and the armor of God prayer almost every day. I have participated in several sessions of deliverance as well as reaffirmed my baptism, and I still seek ministry on a regular basis.

Without the Blessed Mother's help, I probably wouldn't be here writing this book now. I owe her my life.

I started an in-depth religious study on my own. This study, as well as regular prayer, has enabled me to develop a closer relationship to Jesus and our Blessed Mother.

It's really hard to believe that after participating in the evils of the occult for so long, I finally found comfort and solace in something as simple as prayer.

The power of the petition that was carried to Lourdes was astonishing. Our Blessed Mother worked quickly to break me free of Satan's grasp.

One of the most important things to remember is that even the littlest thing, such as using an Ouija board or tarot cards, can put a person on the wrong path and bring the demonic into their life.

Looking back on the whole experience, I recognize certain characteristics that go along with demonic infestation and possession, as well as curses. With all of my experience, I should have recognized this, but I was into the occult and Satan too deeply, so to speak. I had a thirst for the power that the deities and demons were providing to me. I felt as though I was slowly being taken over. During the final stages of this takeover, I felt as if there was a battle going on inside of me between good and evil. There actually was.

This only goes to show that no matter the extent of one's experience in the occult, Satan and his minions will catch up to you and demand his dues.

Once when I was in the Witches Corner, I remember seeing a recruiting poster for a satanic group. This poster had the face of the devil pointing his finger, much like Uncle Sam posters do. The caption underneath the picture read, "Satan Wants You!" How true that statement really is. Regardless of who we are, Satan will try to tempt us because he wants to get his claws on anyone he can. By being involved in the occult, it merely makes his job easier, because the occult offends God.

Although with Mary's intercession I'm no longer under any form of curse that I'm aware of, this still doesn't stop the devil from trying to come back into my life. However, since I've given myself to Jesus and was finally baptized, I now recognize those signs and temptations more easily. Basically, anything negative or anything that attempts to steer you away from Christian belief is an action of the evil one. Most of this is common sense. One must simply avoid the interaction. However, if it persists and you feel yourself being pulled in, it probably isn't a bad idea to visit a Catholic Renewal Center or deliverance ministry or see a priest or pastor.

During these deliverance sessions, which can be compared to mini exorcisms, you are cleansed of most evil and negativity. I still seek the assistance of deliverance ministry as needed.

One thing that I never knew was causing me problems was my past involvement in Freemasonry. I was a Master Mason, but I quit the lodge because I started to feel uncomfortable with their rituals. Little did I know the oaths one takes as a Mason can cause strife. They are essentially bonds with the evil one. Freemasonry gets its roots directly from occult texts.

There is also a great book called *The Healing of Families* by Father Yozefu B. Ssemakula. After completing various worksheets in this book and following the prayers, you can effectively break any curses, especially generational ones. A generational curse is one that has been in your family tree, usually for generations. This curse continues through each new generation. When curses like these are broken, the cursed party usually feels an instant sense of relief, and positive opportunities present themselves.

Also, don't forget the most important part, and that's *prayer*! One good way I found to pray is with visualization. While praying, I imagine myself being pulled into the arms of Jesus or the Blessed Mother. Sometimes I even use Saint Michael. I've found this works well, especially for protection prayers.

The more you pray, the closer you get to God. The closer you get to God, the more upset Satan gets. This is one reason why such holy people as saints have encountered the demonic trying to enter their lives and have experienced the preternatural. So it's essential that you recognize how the evil one works in order to defeat him.

Recently, while driving through our old neighborhood, my son told his mother that he used to experience horrible nightmares and that shadows used to follow him in our past residence. My brother in law, who briefly rented the home, said he witnessed several paranormal events, including windows and doors opening and closing by themselves.

I sincerely hope that others involved in the occult find comfort and solace in putting their lives in God's hands and turning away from the evil grasp of Satan.

PART 2

THE OCCULT AND DEMONIC EXPLAINED

CHAPTER 17

ANGELS, MAGIC, AND THE OCCULT

Angels and Free Will

The word "angel" comes from the Greek "angelos" and means "messenger of God." Angels were created by God in order to serve and praise him. They are divided into nine categories commonly referred to as choirs. The top three choirs are seraphim, cherubim, and thrones, and they are closest to God and heaven. The next three choirs are dominions, powers, and virtues. These angels govern the universe. The last three choirs are closest to humans and are principalities, archangels, and angels.

Angels were (and are) created directly by God and, like humans, were given the gift of free will. During creation, God asked the angels to serve man as well, and some of the angels refused to do so. This is because humans were a lower species than angels, and angels refused to serve them. There was a battle in heaven, and approximately one-third of the angels fell and were cast out of heaven and into hell. This is the reason why the fallen angels hate humanity and seek to destroy it.

Because we have free will, Satan constantly uses temptation to try to get humans to sin and therefore destroy humanity.

One of Satan's best tricks is to influence humans to think that he doesn't exist. This is why denouncing Satan and praising Jesus breaks all ties with all forms of the demonic.

Also interesting to note is the fact that the demonic does *not* have the ability to read our thoughts; however, they can observe our behaviors and make assumptions based on these behaviors.

God allows us to make our own choices, but he also limits the actions of Satan against us.

Even more interesting is the fact that at birth, we are assigned a guardian angel. This angel has the primary task of looking after us by protecting and assisting us until we reach heaven.

Many saints, including Padre Pio, have called upon their guardian angels for help. There is a simple guardian angel prayer in the back of this book.

About the Occult

The term "occult" is derived from the Latin "occultus," meaning hidden or secret. Humanity has had an interest in the unknown for ages.

From early sun worship ceremonies to the more modern rituals of witchcraft, humans continue to delve into the unknown. It is this temptation, which Satan takes advantage of, that can lead to disaster. Dire consequences could come from messing around with what may seem totally innocent; however, when the person desires to seek knowledge through them, this creates the power and the links to the demonic. This is when Satan takes his hold.

The regular practice of flirting with items such as Ouija boards and tarot cards usually leads into a deeper interest in the occult, such as witchcraft.

The information that follows describes how magic spells and curses work and includes a complete breakdown of occult religions and items associated with each religion. I include the item lists because parents, law enforcement, and others may find these especially useful.

History of Magic

Magic is the basis of most occult religions.

Magic began centuries before the start of civilization. The first forms of magic consisted of primitive crude rituals designed to kill animals for food, to prevent death, or to prevent drowning, for example. These primitive magicians then moved to the belief that spirits or souls must be responsible for things like hot and cold, the movements of animals, and the like. These spirits were man's first gods. Leaders of these early religious ceremonies assumed the identity of the god they were worshiping during the ceremony by using movements and dress.

It's believed that early witchcraft came from these early animal cults. For example, in traditional witchcraft, a horned god named Pan is worshiped. During the Middle Ages, witches were gathering herbs and worshiping Pan. Witches argue that they don't worship the devil but instead worship Pan, who holds a close resemblance to the devil. It's believed that witches are worshippers of old pagan animal gods.

The Egyptians refined magical practices that had been used by their ancestors, as well as borrowed practices from older civilizations. From these Egyptian practices, magic words, amulets, talismans, and wax images were incorporated into magic rituals. Mummification was accompanied by magic rituals of unbelievable complexity. These Egyptian rituals heavily influenced western magic. It's believed that ceremonial/ritual magic stemmed from these practices.

In Mesopotamia, early astrology originated in 3,000 BC. Astrology plays a great part in some magical rituals.

Ancient Greece is another place that flourished with magical practices.

The Jewish doctrine of the Kabbalah was also considered to be an early magical working. Kabbalistic ritual was developed in the late Middle Ages.

By the eighteenth century, the first Satanism, which is the actual worship of Satan, occurred. This included the bastardization of Roman Catholic ritual. This is the time period that the infamous Black Mass was first introduced. Most practitioners of witchcraft incorporated satanic rites into their list of ritual workings.

By the late nineteenth century, an occult revival took place in England and France that would eventually find its way into the United States.

CHAPTER 18

HOW AND WHY MAGIC RITUAL WORKS

The world of the occult is owned and controlled by Satan and his minions. This is why curses work. Satan wants to destroy lives regardless if you are the curser or the one being cursed. Satan is pleased with these actions, as both are destructive. In addition to Satan, there are certain prerequisites for successful ritual work.

Components of a Ritual Magic Curse

There's an old saying that goes, "The mind is a powerful thing." This also goes for occult rituals.

In order to cast a spell or curse, one's mind must be programmed, or set to the "right frequency," to induce the right mood for the desired effect. In other words, most ritual work is nothing more than an act to get one's mind into the right mood. The mind is what actually casts the spell. This creates a tie to Satan and his minions as you are seeking something through occult means.

In order to achieve the right mood, all five senses must be highly stimulated in the correct manner to achieve the desired effect. The items used to stimulate each of the five senses are listed below:

- Sight: Environmental setting

- Smell: Incense and oils

- Taste: Wine or herbal concoctions

- Feel: Ritual instruments

- Hearing: Chanting, loud music, or recitation of the spell itself

Magicians divide magic into two subgroups: black and white magic. Black magic involves any act of controlling someone or a deity, spirit, or demon. White magicians tend to believe their magic is innocent and doesn't control others. However, the simple truth is that all forms of magic are bad because everything is controlled by Satan.

In black magic spells, especially curses, magicians try to acquire some item that has the target's DNA on it. In my case, one day I noticed Susan taking my cigarette butts out of the ashtray and pocketing them. This is probably how Steve's sect acquired my DNA to perform their curses. The more personal the item they have, especially with DNA, the tighter the curse will hold. Food can also be ritually cursed to be ingested by the target.

Just as the Roman Catholic Church has sacramentals, such as holy oil, holy water, and incense, occult practitioners have their own forms of occult sacramentals. These consist primarily of concoctions made from herbs or blends of herbal essential oils. The scents or tastes of these concoctions put magicians in the proper mood for their ritual workings. There are books available on how to blend these items to meet the desired purposes. Ritual instruments, such as wands, robes, or knives, all add the desired feel, as do sexual rites if the practitioner is involved in sexual magic.

The next component of magic is sensory overstimulation. These are specific techniques that confuse normal response and force open extrasensory channels. I like to refer to this as "shock stimulation." Some examples of this are extra loud music, masks, or nudeness. Satanists incorporate shock stimulation to a high degree in their rituals.

Most chanted magical spells (like mantras), as well as ritual diagrams, induce the feeling of a meditative state. Power is mobilized by blocking off large areas of sensory response and focusing primarily on one area, sound, or appearance.

Willpower is the final component of ritual magic. Without proper desire or ambition, a ritual is sure to fail.

Curses and Psychic Attacks

The methods one uses to send a curse are endless. Every religious culture has its own form of curses.

At this time, I wish to give the reader a warning. A curse removal, as well as deliverance, should only be performed by qualified experts, such as priests or qualified deliverance ministers. The easiest way to stop a curse is to stay "in grace" with prayer, confession, fasting, etc.

Curses may come from an individual or a whole group depending on the circumstances. The results of a curse on someone's life can include illness, accidents, death, madness, poverty, and suffering, just to name a few. Curses can include friends and family members as they are close to their intended target.

Next, I will name the four classifications of curses, as well as list the various traits associated with them. The curse may be either one type or a blend of several types.

Straight Curse

A straight curse is an action created by a person, usually through some sort of occult ritual, to cause harm to an individual, group, or place. It's called the straight curse because there is simply one direct line to the person or thing being cursed. They are usually left alone to do their job without adding any additional ritual work. Cleverly constructed straight curses may contain trip wires similar to bombs. These trip wires are difficult to dismantle by deliverance ministers. The straight curse may also be tripped or activated when the cursed person does some action. A good example of this is the straight curse in which people are stopped from communicating information. The curse is placed at the beginning during initiation or oath taking and is activated if silence is broken. A good example of this is Freemasonry and its initiation rites. Straight curses usually hit at one time, then gradually lessen as the curse wears off.

Magical/Psychic Attacks

Magical and psychic attacks are a large amount of strong, channeled magic fueled by emotion. The greater the emotion, the nastier the attack. This type of curse differs from the straight curse in that the attack is ongoing instead of being cast only once. The attack form of curse is usually added to other ritual work repeatedly and, instead of lessening, it grows more intense. This form of curse is usually practiced only by occultists. However, it can happen anywhere a large amount of built-up emotion is released subconsciously to another individual.

Demonic Curses

Demonic curses are generally the nastiest curses. This particular curse involves the sending of a demonic entity to attack a particular person, place, or group. This is usually accomplished by a ritual magician. It involves the invocation or summoning of the demon. After the demon is sent to its destination, the result is a demonic infestation, which eventually follows the appropriate stages leading to demonic possession. A demonic curse is easy to identify, as it usually includes preternatural activities associated with demonic infestation. Two other main signs of a demonic curse include the fact that animals attack or are frightened of the cursed person. Also, people act badly toward the cursed individual. Because the demonic curse causes strife in a person's life, other indicators, such as serious accidents, assaults, relationships that fall apart, and marital strife, may also be evident.

Generational Curses

Generational curses are curses that continue from one generation to the next and can include inherited curses during one person's initiation ceremony. This type of curse is especially prevalent in people who have a history of the occult or Freemasonry in their family trees.

CHAPTER 19

SPIRITUALISM

Although the occult can be traced very far back in American history, it was the Spiritualist movement in the 1840's in which the occult saw its first surge through America.

In 1848, Kate Fox and her sisters claimed they heard rapping noises and saw furniture moving in their home, which was said to have been haunted. The Fox sisters soon attempted to communicate with the presence. The tales of the Fox sisters were spread, and, due to heavy public interest, Spiritualism was born.

Spiritualism can be traced back to Europe where writings from authors such as Allan Kardec sparked the public's interest in the occult. The church opposed Spiritualism and stated that the spirit manifestations were attributed to the demonic and the devil.

Spiritualists, however, deny the existence of demons or the devil. They believe that when we die, we are all basically reincarnated; however, some souls remain earthbound and become spirits. It is further believed that Spiritualist mediums hold the ability to communicate with these spirits and souls and send them onto their next life. The mediums are also believed to communicate with other higher powers, including angels. According to the manual of the National Spiritualism Association: "A Spiritualist is one who believes, as a part of his or her religion, in the communication between this and the spirit world by means of mediumship, and who endeavors to mold his or her character in accordance with the highest teachings derived from such communion." People usually get involved with Spiritualism for one of two reasons: loss of a loved one or curiosity.

At Spiritualist churches and meetings, the medium usually sits in a chair at the front of the room and gives messages from the dead. They may also walk directly up to someone and give them intimate details about a past loved one or themselves. In Acts 16:16, the Bible cautions us that Satan and his minions have the uncanny knack of knowing these types of things about us from observing our behavior. In Leviticus 20:27, we are strongly warned against the use of mediums.

There are two types of mediumship. One is mental, and the other is physical.

Mental mediumship involves the medium communicating with the spirit and relaying the message back to the audience or person. The medium can contact the spirit world to deliver these messages in two ways. One is by clairvoyance, which is the ability to see spirits. (Outside of a Spiritualist context, the term clairvoyance also means to possess psychic abilities.) The other is clairaudience, which is the ability to hear spirits. Some mediums have only one of these abilities, while some have both.

A physical medium allows the spirit to take over one's body. This is extremely dangerous, as you can imagine. The common new age term for physical mediumship is channeling.

Spiritualists also claim to be able to communicate with angels. In 2 Corinthians 11:14, it is explained that Satan can masquerade as an angel of light.

Three main items are associated with Spiritualism and spirit communication: the Ouija board, pendulum, and spirit trumpet.

The Ouija board is a board with letters and a pointer, or planchette. As someone touches the planchette, it moves to the appropriate letters to spell out the spirit's message.

A pendulum is an item suspended from a string or chain. When asked a question it will sway to one side or the other to answer the question. Modern versions of pendulums often include a semiprecious stone on a chain.

A spirit trumpet is a device through which spirits supposedly can communicate and is usually used only by mediums.

Spiritualist camps are located all over the United States. One of the most popular is located in Camp Chesterfield, Indiana.

Spiritualists sometimes engage in table rapping. This is spirit communication in which the spirit raps on a table or wall. So many raps for yes and so many for no. The Fox sisters used this type of communication during their attempts to communicate with the spirit or spirits.

CHAPTER 20

ALEISTER CROWLEY: THE GRANDFATHER OF MODERN OCCULTISM

No one person has had such an influence on modern occultism as Aleister Crowley. Therefore, no book on the dangers of the occult would be complete without mentioning him.

Aleister Crowley was born on October 12, 1875, to a Quaker family in England. The Crowleys had run a brewery for two hundred years prior to Aleister's birth. Crowley made several claims that he was of noble descent, as well as that he was born with the characteristics of a Buddha. Crowley's father left the Quakers and joined the Brethren, a more extreme fundamentalist faith, while Aleister was young. When young Aleister misbehaved, his mother referred to him as The Beast (from the book of Revelation), a title that Crowley would proclaim later in life. Young Crowley developed a keen dislike against members of organized Christian religion. His father died when Crowley was just eleven, which sent young Aleister into total rebellion.

Crowley entered Cambridge's Trinity College in 1895 in moral sciences. Stubborn Crowley never attended mandatory student chapel nor would he eat with his classmates. He instead paid the kitchen staff to bring meals to his room.

Crowley loved reading and writing poetry. His hobbies also included mountain climbing, and he set records around the world.

His interest in the occult led him to join the Hermetic Order of the Golden Dawn. The Golden Dawn was founded in 1887 as a splinter group of a Rosicrucian sect. Among its members was Samuel MacGregor Mathers, a master of occult studies. After Crowley's entrance into the organization, he proceeded to master all of the material. However, Crowley claimed that a more potent magic could be harnessed through the use of sex and drugs. Mathers disagreed, and so a horrible magical war started. In the end, Mathers was supposedly killed by an entity that Crowley conjured up.

Still thirsting for more occult studies, Crowley drifted away from the Golden Dawn and traveled the world studying yoga, Hinduism, and Buddhism.

It was during these travels that Crowley met his future wife, Rose Kelly. After getting married, the two honeymooned in Egypt, where Crowley performed magical rituals in the King's Chamber of the Great Pyramid. It was at this time that Rose supposedly went into some type of trance state and spoke of how the Egyptian god Horus wanted to communicate with Crowley.

Crowley wanted verification that Rose was in fact communicating with Horus, so he took Rose, who had no knowledge of Egyptian mythology, to a museum. Once inside the museum, Crowley asked Rose to point out an image of Horus. Rose then pointed to a wooden tablet (Exhibit Number 666), and much to Crowley's surprise, Rose correctly identified Horus. Rose then described a magical ritual Crowley was supposed to perform.

Crowley performed the ritual. The result was Crowley's *The Book of the Law*, a book dictated to Rose by a demon named Aiwass, Crowley's supposed guardian angel. From the book came one of Crowley's most notable phrases: "Do what thou wilt shall be the whole of the law."

Upon returning to England, Rose became pregnant with Crowley's daughter. Crowley then took Rose and his new infant daughter to China. While returning from China, Crowley took a separate route from his family. He discovered after returning to England that his daughter had died of typhoid and that Rose had become an alcoholic.

Crowley left Rose and wrote *The Book of Lies* (1912), which was an exercise in writing ninety-three chapters of magical instruction. One of these chapters caught the eye of Theodor Reuss, head of the Ordo Templi Orientis. This chapter exposed the OTO's primary secret. Reuss then appointed Crowley the British head of the OTO. Crowley chose the magical name Baphomet (taken after the goat-horned god).

Crowley moved to America in 1914 after World War I broke out in England. While living in New Hampshire, Crowley achieved the rank of magus. During his induction ceremony, he baptized a frog, named it Jesus Christ, and then crucified it. Crowley had already spent all of his inheritance and hoped to sell some of his works in America. He also hoped to establish an OTO body in America.

Crowley spent the rest of his life in a world of magic, perversion, and drugs.

He met Leah Hirsig, and the two left for Cefalù, Italy, in order to establish a magical commune. They named their commune The Abbey of Thelema. When it was discovered that the abbey was the scene of perverse sexual orgies, Mussolini expelled Crowley in 1923. The London press published several negative articles regarding what went on at the abbey in Italy. The article dubbed Crowley, "The Wickedest Man in the World." One member of the commune died after supposedly drinking black cat blood.

Crowley believed that perverse sexual practice and drug use destroyed the mind barriers of any sense of morality. This, in turn, enabled the conscience, deprived of a sense of morals or law, to come under the influence of powerful demons.

Crowley then settled in Paris with his new secretary, Israel Regardie. He returned to Hastings in 1947, where he died peacefully of respiratory illness. He was nearly broke.

Although Crowley never considered himself a Satanist, as he was a ritual magician, his writings helped shape Satanism and the occult in America. Crowley is rumored to have heavily influenced Wicca as he supposedly wrote most of the material for Gerald Gardner, a Crowley follower and the founder of modern Wicca.

In California during the 1940s, a group of Thelemites, a nickname for Crowley followers, operated the only active OTO body in the world. Today several bodies of the OTO are scattered all over the world. Almost every occult practitioner has in some way been influenced by Crowley. Crowley's material is still in print and highly sought after by modern occultists. Although ritual/ceremonial magic was around for hundreds of years, Crowley is responsible for bringing it to the modern occult practitioner.

As you read in the chapter on curses, ritual/ceremonial/high magic—no matter which name it goes by—is one of the most dangerous forms of the occult because its primary function is to summon entities (demons) for various purposes.

CHAPTER 21

WITCHCRAFT AND WICCA

There are three primary types of witchcraft. Each is described in this chapter.

Gardnerian Witchcraft/Wicca

The first type of witchcraft is Gardnerian witchcraft, or Gardnerian Wicca. Gerald B. Gardner, a follower of Aleister Crowley, was an archeologist, nudist, and occultist. Gardner claimed that there were "witches" in Britain practicing not an anti-Christian religion, but a two-thousand-year-old nature religion, Wicca. In this religion there were two supreme gods, one male and one female. The female, called the Mother Goddess, ruled the earth, and the male, called Pan, was the ruler of sun and fertility.

A paper written by Gardner and published in *Ripley's Believe It or Not!* disclosed that Gardner blended several types of occultism, including Aleister Crowley's rituals, in order to produce the religion of Wicca. Gardner's writings about Wicca's rituals and practices were almost totally modern in nature and in no way were comparative to two-thousand-year-old pagan rites. In addition, Gardner had already published a novel titled *High Magic's Aid*. It's heavily rumored among occult practitioners that Gardner contracted with Aleister Crowley to initiate the writings of Wicca. Portions of the Great Rite ceremony are right out of Crowley's book *Liber AL vel Legis*. Evidence has turned up in the last twenty years that suggests Gardner was a member of Crowley's occult society, the OTO. Thus any claim of Gardner's about the age of Wicca is highly suspect. This puts Wicca in an extremely bad light, as most Wiccans openly condemn anything having to do with Aleister Crowley or the dark arts. If Aleister Crowley was involved in the origins and writings of modern Wicca, rest assured that Wicca was designed as a stepping-stone to other darker occult practices.

Many Wiccans now believe that Gardner's story appears to be a fraud but say that Gardner was channeling or tapping into some sort of ancient memories from a past life. Wiccans go by the rede "and it harm none, do what ye will," which is basically the same as Aleister Crowley's "Do what thou wilt shall be the whole of the law." Just as Crowley did, some Wiccans place a heavy emphasis on sexual magic, as it's believed that the energy arising from sexual pleasure can be harnessed into ritual work.

Wiccans generally believe in two types of magic, white and black. White is supposedly good magic that comes from the right-hand path of the Tree of Life, while black magic is generally used to influence or control people and comes from the left-hand path of the Tree of Life.

Wiccans believe that the pentagram/pentacle in its right-side-up position with one point upward is a symbol of white or good magic and that an inverted star with two points up is a symbol for black or negative magic. Most Wiccans do not condone black magic; however, after the second degree in most initiations, the inverted pentagram is mostly used.

Wiccans cast spells using the natural elements of earth, air, fire, and water. Each element is believed to have their own special spirits, as does everything in nature.

Wiccans don't believe in Satan, as they say he's merely a figment of Christian thinking and religion.

The term "Wicca" today is generally used by most practicing witches, even those who practice various types of witchcraft. Generally, Wiccans are a peaceful, nature-loving people. However, I believe Wicca is simply a stepping-stone into other harder and darker occult practices, as it is still Satan's work.

Alexandrian or Traditional Witchcraft

The second type is Alexandrian, or traditional, witchcraft. Alex Sanders founded Alexandrian witchcraft claiming to have higher degrees than Gardnerian witchcraft. Sanders claimed to have known and studied under Aleister Crowley, and he incorporated Crowley's ritual style into his rituals. Therefore, Alexandrian witchcraft is generally a blend of traditional witchcraft and ceremonial magic.

Dianic Witchcraft

The third type of witchcraft is Dianic witchcraft, which is feminist witchcraft. In most forms of witchcraft, witches invoke the Mother Goddess and her male consort, the Horned God (Pan). The Mother Goddess is also known as the Triple Goddess because of the three phases of the moon: waxing, waning, and full. Due to the many different ways of invocation and practicing styles, the goddess may be invoked using a variety of different names, including:

- Aphrodite
- Hecate
- Astaroth
- Isis
- Astarte
- Lilith
- Ceres
- Luna
- Diana
- Venus

The male counterpart is, naturally, representative of the opposite pole or the sun. His names are:

- Cernunnos
- Osiris
- Hades
- Pan
- Horus
- Thor
- Odin

Pan is the most popular of these names.

Witches do not believe in demons or hell, as they think of these as purely Christian belief.

Witches celebrate many holidays. They are as follows:

Holiday	Date	Purpose
Samhain	October 31	Honor the dead and the deities of transition and afterlife
Yule	December 21	Mark rebirth of the sun god
Candlemas	February 2	Promote healing
Vernal Equinox	March 20 or 21	Celebrate of fertility
Beltane or May Eve	April 30	Celebrate Baal

Holiday	Date	Purpose
Summer Solstice	June 20 or 21	Celebrate transformation
Lammas Eve	July 31	Celebrate the beginning of the harvest
Autumnal Equinox	September 21 or 22	Celebrate the end of the harvest

While the holidays listed are mostly on the eves, the holiday may be celebrated on the following day.

Wiccans practice their craft either solitarily or in a group with a coven.

Wiccans have a lot of paraphernalia associated with their rites. Enclosed is a list of various paraphernalia associated with Wiccan covens and practitioners:

- Knife: Commonly referred to as an athame. It is primarily used for the casting of magic circles. These may either be colored black or white, representing the masculine and feminine.

- Bowl of salt and water: Water representing the element water and salt for earth or purification

- Bell: For ringing at the needed time in a ritual; also for summoning

- Cord: For binding spells as well as to get proper measurement of a nine-foot circle

- Chalice: For drinking wine

- Censer: For burning incense of herbs

- Stones and crystals: For power source

- Incense and herbs: For burning

- Oils: For anointing

- Pentacle: Used during ritual

- Robe: Primary dress for occultists

CHAPTER 22

HIGH OR CEREMONIAL MAGIC

High or ceremonial magic is perhaps one of the most dangerous forms of the occult. This occult operation involves the direct invocation or summoning of demons. These demons can be invoked for a variety of reasons, not limited to cursing another, seeking wealth, seeking love, or for any other reason one could possibly think of.

The instructions for invocation can be found in numerous occult works, most of which were produced in the Middle Ages and Renaissance. Modern occult magicians have produced modern versions of these early texts that are easier to follow.

During the late 1500s a mathematician named John Dee supposedly received communication from demonic entities. He wrote these communications down. They are now known as the Enochian system of magic, which is gaining popularity.

So how do these invocations work, you ask? The magician must follow meticulous instructions from the texts. These instructions include the casting of a detailed circle. A figure of the demon usually appears within the smoke of the incense or within a scrying mirror. These texts also contain detailed charts for the days of the conjurations, as well as the appropriate colors and, in most cases, a listing of the occult sacramentals used. High magic is definitely no place for the occult novice. A typical novice mistake is to fail to banish, or discharge, the demon once it is invoked. Most novices leave the circle after not receiving any results. This provides a large door for the demon to enter through at any time, which could be minutes, hours, or even months later. One thing is for certain: if you summon the devil or his minions, he most definitely will arrive at some time to try to distance you from our Lord and wreak havoc. *He will not fail to accept your invitation!!*

Ceremonial magic, or high magic, gets its roots from ancient Egypt.

Sex is used in a wide variety of rituals. At the moment of orgasm, certain ritual words are uttered as part of the invocation process. Enochian magic has been known to contain a vast amount of sexual rituals.

One modern danger is that some of the occult texts, which have been rewritten to be easy to follow, are finding their way into the hands of some of the occult's most inexperienced members, the new agers. Even more frightening is that these texts have been interpreted word for word and thus commonly refer to the demons as *angels* and fail to properly state their fallen angel status. Numerous new age books on the market refer to angels. Therefore, some new agers actually think they're invoking holy angels instead of demons.

High magicians sometimes grow accustomed to preternatural activity as it is usually present during a severe demonic infestation. Magicians have described such events as rapping coming from furniture, foul odors, and hearing voices but finding no one there.

Some modern ceremonial magicians include Aleister Crowley and Éliphas Lévi. Aleister Crowley initiated the spelling of "magick" with a letter *k* on the end in order to tell it apart from stage magic.

The implements of ceremonial magic are expensive and hard to find but still can be obtained from occult supply stores. These include:

- Robes
- Incense
- Oils
- Wand
- Sword

- Knife
- Texts
- Incense burners
- Altar sigil
- Scrying mirror

The writing and art of ceremonial magic are intricate, as are the texts themselves.

Practitioners of ceremonial magic use it in conjunction with other religions or simply practice it by itself, as it contains no specific religious beliefs and is geared solely toward the practice of magic and the summoning of demons.

CHAPTER 23

SATANISM

Tons of information is available on Satanism, so for instructional purposes, I will stick to the basic information.

During the 1960s and 1970s, the occult exploded onto the American cultural scene. In this era, Roman Polanski's movie *Rosemary's Baby* was a huge box office success. Anton LaVey, who founded the Church of Satan in 1966, is quoted as saying that the film *Rosemary's Baby* did for Satanism what *The Birth of a Nation* did for the Ku Klux Klan. LaVey then penned the Satanic Bible in 1969.

I should mention at this point that most occultists find the Catholic religion of great importance as it can be traced directly back to Jesus's apostles. Most occultists know this, and that is why Catholic churches are burglarized and Catholic religious implements are stolen. Satanists steal these objects for the use of desecration. It is believed that the bastardization of these sacred objects brings them closer to Satan. Communion wafers are especially sought after.

Perhaps the most recognized ritual of Satanism is the Black Mass. This ritual serves three specific purposes:

1. To invert Christian elements, which brings about satanic powers.

2. To build magical energy.

3. To liberate initiated Satanists from the Catholic Church's dogma. During the Black Mass everything is done in reverse order of the Catholic mass. Satanists walk backward while casting the circle. The Lord's Prayer is usually read backward. Black Masses are held at night because less people are praying at that hour, so the prayers don't interfere with the rituals.

Zeena LaVey, Anton's daughter, disowned her father and his belief system. She eventually joined another satanic organization known as the Temple of Set. In 1975, Church of Satan member Michael Aquino invoked Satan in order to receive further instructions for operating the Church of Satan apart from LaVey. According to Aquino, Satan came to him as Set, the Egyptian equivalent of Satan, and the Temple of Set was born. The Temple of Set is a secretive satanic organization, and they are very selective in their membership standards.

Satanic belief and Satanists as a whole can be classified into two main categories: theological and nontheological. Theological Satanists believe in an actual deity, whether it be Satan, Set, Beelzebub, etc. Nontheological Satanists DO NOT believe in any deity. Nontheological Satanism is more or less atheistic in nature. These types of Satanists believe in indulging as much as possible in the seven deadly sins.

Satanists can be classified further into two more classes: solitary or group. In other words, either the Satanist is practicing by themselves or they are a member of a group. Literally thousands of groups are located all over the world. Most Satanists and their groups are law-abiding citizens; however, some are not.

Some satanic organizations are tied into neo-Nazi organizations or idealism. Adolf Hitler was interested in the occult, most notably, in astrology. Hitler borrowed from an occultist named Madame Blavatsky. Blavatsky's book, *The Secret Doctrine*, which Hitler followed, spoke of a monastery hidden under a mountain in Tibet. Blavatsky claimed that a supreme race of people known as Aryans lived there and that the Aryan race was over a million years old. She associated the Aryans with the swastika—a Tibetan symbol meaning the sun and good fortune. Hitler made the swastika the sign of the Nazis.

Occultists, especially Satanists, have picked up on this belief system.

On August 8, 1988, Zeena LaVey and others held a large group rally that celebrated the murder of Sharon Tate and an end to the corrupt era of the 1960s.

The number "88" is often found around satanic graffiti. This means "Heil Hitler" as H is the eighth letter of the alphabet.

The 1980s saw what is commonly referred to as Satanic Panic. Rumors spread of a vast satanic organized criminal network that was supposedly involved in everything from child ritual abuse to ritual murders. These rumors were heavily fueled by shows like *Geraldo*, which flaunted a wide variety of so-called occult guests and experts.

The simple truth is that there was no vast underground satanic network. Although satanic ritual abuse and illegal satanic activities occur, these events are rarer than most people think. Also, although I consider Satanism to be spiritually and mentally destructive, the truth is that most Satanists are law-abiding citizens. Most crimes involving animal sacrifices or remains are lumped into the Satanism category but are actually part of Santería or Palo Mayombe, which we will discuss later.

The following are dates of satanic holidays:

- Imbolc: February 1

- Ostara: March 20–23

- Beltane: May 1

- Litla: June 20–23

- Lughnasadh: August 1

- Mabon: September 20–23

- Samhain: October 31

- Yule: December 21–23

The most important of the holidays is the member's birthday.

The following are items used during satanic ceremonies:

- Altar cloth: Usually with an upside-down star or pentagram

- Knife: For casting circles

- Bell: For beginning ritual

- Candles: For spells and atmosphere

- Chalice: To drink from

- Gong: For beginning ritual

- Mirror: For scrying and summoning demons

- Oils: For anointing body or candles

- Salt: For controlling demons

- Staff: Used in rituals

- Sword: Used in rituals

- Wand: Used in rituals

CHAPTER 24

THE AFRO-CARIBBEAN RELIGIONS

There are several Afro-Caribbean religions. I will give brief descriptions of each one. In my opinion, these religions contain some of the nastiest demons. This is probably due to the fact that each religion requires every member to voluntarily allow possession to take place and usually involve the sacrifice of animals as well.

Santería

Santería can be found in most highly populated and ethnic areas of the United States. Although Santería's roots are of African descent, the religion evolved once its adherents were enslaved and brought to America. In America, enslaved Africans were forced to practice Christianity, mostly Catholicism. They wanted to practice their old religious beliefs, so they combined these old beliefs with Catholicism. This is why Catholic saint statues and other items are usually found on altars and sites of these African religions.

Santería has seven primary deities (or orishas) as well as one chief deity named Olorun. The seven primary orishas are also known as the Seven African Powers. There are lower deities as well. Here's is a list of the primary orishas:

- Eleguá: Controls crossroads, gates, and doors and allows communication with other orishas. Catholic equivalent in Santería is Saint Anthony.

- Obatala: Father of all creation, source of energy, wisdom, and purity. Catholic equivalent in Santería is Our Lady of Mercedes.

- Chango: Controls thunder, lightning, and fire. Usually invoked in malevolent sorcery. The Catholic equivalent in Santería is Saint Barbara.

- Oshun: Money, sex, love. The Catholic equivalent in Santería is Our Lady of Charity.

- Yemaya: Mother of Santería. Owns the seas. The Catholic equivalent in Santería is Our Lady of Regla.

- Babalú-Ayé: Patron of the sick. The Catholic equivalent in Santería is Saint Lazarus.

- Oggun: Warrior deity usually invoked in malevolent sorcery. The Catholic equivalent in Santería is Saint Peter.

The main requirement for initiation into Santería is first to be baptized in a Catholic church. The second step is selecting a guardian orisha, and the third step is what is referred to as making the saint. The final process of making a saint is expensive, usually costing the initiate thousands of dollars. Some travel to Cuba instead of staying in the United States because it's cheaper there.

As in most of the Afro-Caribbean religions, the final step of initiation involves cutting the initiate's head by the Santero (Santería priest). After cutting the head, the Santero places an herbal concoction into the cut. This concoction is supposed to bind one to the chosen orisha.

A typical Santería ceremony includes drums, chanting, incense, and candles. After the invocation of the orisha is complete, the drummers alter the rhythm in order to usher in a new orisha.

These religions usually involve animal sacrifices. Santería is no exception. A 1993 Supreme Court decision in Hialeah, Florida, allows for the religious sacrifice of animals so long as the animals aren't made to suffer.

Most of the supplies for Santería can be found in stores called botanicas, which are usually located in heavily populated Hispanic neighborhoods.

Santa Muerte

Although of Hispanic origin and not African, Santa Muerte is rapidly growing and therefore deserves mention. Its statues and supplies are usually found in botanicas.

Santa Muerte, or holy death as it is sometimes called, is a statue resembling the Grim Reaper holding a sickle and a globe. These statues come in a wide variety of sizes and colors. The colors represent specific purposes for the statue:

- White: Protection from black magic

- Red: Love

- Black: Malevolent sorcery

- Green: Money

These statues are usually used for protection from law enforcement. The whole concept of Santa Muerte is believed to be based on a Mexican folk saint, but no one is sure of its origins. The religion is popular in Mexico.

Voodoo

Voudon, commonly called Voodoo, is rooted in African religions. Like Santería, it too came to America via the slave trade. Just like Santería, enslaved Africans incorporated Catholicism into their magical belief system.

A Voodoo male priest is called a houngan, and a female priestess is known as a mambo.

Much like Santería's Eleguá, Voodoo has Papa Legba, which serves as communication between the priest or priestess and the deities (loa). Other loa include:

- Agwé: God of the sea

- Erzulie: Female goddess of love and sex

- Dambalah: Serpent deity

- Baron Samedi: Guardian of the cemeteries

A Voodoo ceremony is much like a Santería ceremony, except it uses a pillar pole in the center of the temple to bring in energy.

Possession in Voodoo is sometimes referred to as "riding the horse." These spirits usually enter through the back of the neck.

Animal sacrifices are usually chickens.

An initiation into Voodoo usually involves three steps: The first is a cleansing process. Second is a fire ritual, and third is a study of the loas, dance rhythms, and symbols, which are commonly called veves.

Hoodoo

Hoodoo isn't really a religion in itself but is part of its parent religion of Voodoo. Hoodoo is best described as Voodoo without religious ritual.

Rituals are usually performed for love, money, success, etc. Root doctors fall into this category as do some psychics, especially those located in the southern United States, that dabble with candles, oils, herbs, incenses, etc.

The same ritual items found in Voodoo will usually be found in Hoodoo. I like to think of Hoodoo as "fast food" Voodoo, as the rituals are usually simplified.

Palo Mayombe

On July 17, 2000, Margaret Ramirez, seventy-four, was struck dead by a car while crossing the street near her New York City apartment. Her death led police to her home, which some police have described as a chamber of horrors. One of the most frightening things was a dead baby girl inside of a jar. Perhaps Margaret Ramirez's demons finally caught up with her. You see, she was a practitioner of the Afro-Cuban religion known as Palo Mayombe.

Palo Mayombe is known in the world of the occult as being the most potent and nastiest form of black magic. It's sometimes described to unsuspecting initiates as "unsanctified Santería." Followers of Palo believe that they can use human body parts to contact and control the spirits of the dead. These spirits are then compelled to do the practitioner's bidding, usually at the service of evil.

One police officer stated in the Ramirez case, "When you deal with Palo Mayombe, you're dealing usually with the devil himself!"

Ramirez's son, fifty-four, and Ramirez were probably using the baby girl's remains in rituals. Ramirez's son has denied any involvement whatsoever, and he is a resident of a locked psychiatric ward in a New York VA hospital. Police also found two skulls (one was a child's) and a ceremonial cauldron called a nganga pot. One Palo priest from New York dismissed Ramirez as a novice who dabbled in dangerous black magic when she should have stuck to reading tarot cards.

Palo Mayombe, usually called Palo by its practitioners, is a mysterious and secretive religion that originated in the Congo of Africa before enslaved Africans brought it with them to Cuba. The word Palo means stick. This refers to the different types of exotic woods that are inserted into the nganga pot. While shrouded in secrecy in the United States, Palo is openly practiced in Cuba. You can hardly find an English language book on the subject.

Palo consists of two elements: herbs and the dead. At the center of Palo practice is the nganga pot. It is in this pot that the demons live. The demons are slaves to the owner of the pot.

A nganga pot is constructed usually of stones, Palo sticks, herbs, graveyard dirt, waters, shells, and sacrificed animal blood. Bones—usually a human neck bone, commonly referred to as the atlas bone—are placed in the pot in order to produce a nfumbe, or spirit of the dead in its essence. These bones are usually ordered from medical supply houses via the internet, or in the worst-case scenario, stolen from graves. An animal or human skull may also be added to the nganga pot.

A bamboo stick is also used for nganga pots. River water, sea water, and mercury can be found inside of this hollow bamboo stick. This stick is sealed with wax and cement at both ends. The stick is used to stir the demon and to help keep it stable.

These demons are tortured by the owner and taught to obey the practitioner.

Ngangas are usually kept in an outdoor shed called a nsu nganga.

Different elemental demons inhabit the ngangas. One common elemental demon is Lucero, which is similar to Eleguá in Santería. Lucero statues are made of stone or clay and have a cowrie shell face. They are usually found sitting next to the nganga pot. The demons inside of nganga pots need to be "fed" or have sacrifices. Sacrifices for Lucero includes goats, black roosters, dogs, and guinea hens. Following is a list of the other demons and their sacrifices:

- Siete Rayos: A seven rays spirit associated with war. This is equivalent to Santería's Chango. Its color is red, and it is fed red roosters and water turtles.

- Zarabanda: Rules over iron. It is fed black dogs, black dog bones, and black roosters. Its favorite things include spikes, machetes, and knives.

- Mama Sholan: Rules over rivers, money, and love. It is fed guinea hens and honey.

- Centella Ndoki: Rules over cemeteries and is fed black cats.

In order to summon the demons, the Palero or (Palo priest) draws the sign of the demon on the floor and chants the appropriate chant. Small piles of incense mixed with gunpowder are lit around the nganga. The practitioner then makes their wishes known.

Initiates into Palo wear clothes that have been buried in a graveyard. The initiate is also cut on the head (called "scratching" in Palo), then blood from the initiate is dripped into the nganga for binding the initiate to the demon.

Although Palo practitioners claim to use legal, quick kill techniques for their sacrifices, most practitioners torture these animals prior to killing them because they believe this raises the sacrifice's energy level.

The most noted Palo case occurred just over the United States border in Mexico. The case involved Adolfo de Jesús Constanzo, who was a Mexican drug kingpin that led a ring of drug runners. (Palo practitioners' services are often sought out by drug dealers.) Constanzo used a mix of Palo and Santería and worked spells in order to protect his drug trade.

One day, a member of Constanzo's gang blew past a police roadblock with a load of dope. He thought he was protected by Constanzo's magic powers, which would make him invisible to law enforcement. From information provided by him, Constanzo's ranch was searched and human bodies were found. Constanzo was feeding some of these bodies to his nganga. One American was found among the dead: Mark Kilroy, a medical student who had been kidnapped while on spring break, was among the victims. Ironically, Constanzo died with his lover during a police shootout. Palo priests can supposedly cause mental illness and death as a result of their rituals.

CHAPTER 25

THE DEMONIC

For this chapter I am relying mostly on my past experiences relating to the occult and demonic. I still feel the information I have could be of help in assisting those involved in such issues. This chapter is not meant as a total guide to dealing with these problems. If you are experiencing problems that you believe are related to the demonic, please consult your local parish clergy or nearest Catholic Charismatic Renewal.

I also want to mention these two terms: supernatural and preternatural. The term supernatural refers to phenomena related to God, such as stigmata, miracles, etc., while preternatural refers to phenomena associated with the evil one such as demonic attacks.

People may encounter three types of spirits during their lifetime. They are:

- Holy or divine spirits

- Holy angelic or demonic spirits

- Human spirits

For the purposes of this book we will only be dealing with the demonic. For your information, human spirits are spirits of human beings who have died and are commonly referred to as ghosts.

Demonic Spirits

Almost every major religious belief system has its own version of demons and the demonic—they are not only a Christian belief. Although demons can make their presence known to anyone of any religious faith, Catholics are more vulnerable to this as Catholicism can be traced directly back to the apostles (or is apostolic, as we say in the Nicene Creed). The evil one hates anything that is closely associated with God. This closeness to God is why saints usually encounter the demonic at some point in their lives.

Saint Padre Pio, for instance, was tormented by demons throughout his life. He would say, "Long live Jesus," and the demons would banish.

Demon comes from the Greek word "daimon," meaning intelligent. Many of today's demons started out as old pagan gods. As stated earlier, Catholics believe that one-third of the angels fell from heaven and rebelled with Satan against God.

Demons use temptation as their primary source of disruption. This is especially true of the occult, such as the temptation to use Ouija boards or tarot cards. The evil one causes temptation by arousing emotions such as anger, lust, hatred, and fear. For an occult practitioner, the evil one will usually use these emotions then place a possible occult solution into the mix, such as casting a spell or using the Ouija board for guidance.

Just like the hierarchy of heavenly angels, there is also a hierarchy of demons. Satan is at the top of the hierarchy, then high-ranking demons next, and lower demons at the bottom closest to humans. All demons lie and try to give the impression that they're high ranking. Perhaps the only traits of a high-ranking demon are the ability to move or destroy religious items or having a biblical name.

They will also try to use ghosts to do their bidding. This is another reason why ghosts are usually present at demonic infestations. For example, demons have been known to appear as the apparition of a little girl who is lost or a deceased family member. This is meant to appeal to human emotion in the hopes that a person feels sorry for the little girl's ghost and opens up a line of communication with them. These apparitions will be altered or appear to be missing something.

Demons like to remain dormant after a house blessing to give the impression that they're gone, only to return later with a vengeance.

Demonic power is real and mocks the unlimited power of God.

Demons invoked by Afro-Caribbean religious practices are some of the nastiest because they have had longer time to root as they are invited into a person by voluntary possession.

There are four primary measures to take against the evil one and demonic influences. They are as follows:

- Use of Holy Sacraments: Especially the confession of sins. Why carry around human emotions when you can rid yourself of them by going to confession. The evil one, as stated above, loves to stir up these emotions.

- Prayer: In particular the Our Father and Hail Mary. The demonic also hates the rosary.

- Fasting or giving something up.

- Use of sacramentals: Holy water, Saint Benedict medals, holy oil, blessed salt, etc.

The goal of the evil one and demons is to simply destroy humankind. They usually try to do so in four stages.

Four Stages of Demonic Attacks

1. Oppression

The first stage of a demonic attack—called oppression—starts with attacks on a person's exterior life, such as illness, relationship problems, financial problems, etc. The demon takes control of the victim's will. This can lead to an internal or psychological breakdown, which occurs when demons have gained the right to interact with a person. The characteristics of demonic infestation are sometimes present as well during this stage. The victim may suffer physical attacks. There is usually some sort of occult interest and drugs or alcohol. A person may also become oppressed if the demonic was present for the same problem during a previous generation. This is usually known as a generational curse and can usually be broken by obtaining deliverance ministry from clergy or prayer ministers.

2. Obsession

The obsession stage involves demonic attacks on a person's interior life. These may cause the person to be obsessed with negative or evil thoughts that torment them. The victim may obsess about negative things in their life such as drugs, alcohol, the occult, abuse, etc. Nightmares, hallucinations, and suicidal tendencies may occur. The victim may feel as though they are going insane.

3. Infestation

The term infestation is used when demonic activity is connected to an object or location. This involves the infiltration of one's home or building site by demons. This usually occurs as the demons are invited in and have obtained the right to manifest. At this stage the demons are around and make their presence known by acting on our external senses of sight, hearing, and touch. Foul odors may also present themselves. Oppression and obsession may still be occurring while this stage occurs.

4. Possession

The ultimate goal of the infesting demons is to take over or enter a person's body and destroy them. Possession sometimes ends in suicide or murder. Possession is extremely rare, and when it does occur, it usually involves the occult in some way.

I would like to go further into the two latter terms, infestation and possession.

Demonic Infestation

Infestation is usually caused by one or more of the following factors:

- Someone has attempted to communicate with the demon or obtain occult knowledge or has simply brought the occult into their lives. Please note that the demon will stay as long as someone attempts to continue to communicate with it.

- A demon is summoned to appear at a specific location through occult ritual practice. The demon then stays until is it exorcized. I would like to add that during this stage, the demon may appear quickly or at a later time. Time is *not* a factor of the demon's appearance. It will appear when it *wants* to and only then.

- A curse or psychic attack occurs. Demons can be summoned to attack a person through various occult rituals.

- Someone brings a cursed or demonic object into the home or a particular place.

- Excessive abuse of any kind is happening in the home.

What follows are various signs of a demonic infestation:

- Activity gradually escalates

- Activity occurs around 3 a.m. or 6 a.m.

- Three knocks or raps are heard on walls or doors

- Activity causes distractions from a regular healthy life

- Fighting, strife, or arguing in home

- Foul odors

- Scratching sounds on walls similar to sound of mice

- Manipulation or destruction of religious objects

- Suicidal tendencies

- Visible dark masses or shadows of any size

- Violent tendencies of people in home

- Fascination or obsession with death

- Vivid nightmares

- Physical attacks

- Causes hatred toward Christian beliefs

- Demon uses Christian names when communicating, such as Peter, Paul, Mark, etc.

- Feeling of pressure in certain areas as if under a waterfall

- Nausea

- Distorted or muffled unexplained sounds

- One person in family seems to be singled out by the activity

- Cold spots in certain areas

- Mimicking of family member's voices

- Things occurring in threes (to mock the Holy Trinity)

Of course, every case is different. These are the most common signs of demonic infestation. Please understand that in most cases, you must have several of the signs, and even then, it still may not turn out to be demonic infestation. Solving these types of situations are best left to clergy or deliverance ministers. In most cases a simple house blessing by a priest gets rid of the problem.

Beware of anyone who charges money to get rid of your problem or provides an exorcism for cash. These people are merely charlatans. Also beware of any new age or occult solution to the problem, as what usually happens is the demon lies dormant then comes back with a fury. Such practices tend to give the demon or demons more energy than getting rid of them.

A good common practice is to cleanse your house with holy water, blessed oil, and blessed salt. Sprinkle holy water in the four corners and center of every room while reciting the Lord's Prayer. Trace a crucifix with the oil above every doorway while reciting the Lord's Prayer. You may then sprinkle the blessed salt thoroughly around the room. The salt may be eaten by members of the family as well. I'm aware of one deliverance minister who buys salt packets from a local wholesale club and then has them blessed. She always carries them with her in the event she or someone else needs it. Only use sacraments that are obtained from a Catholic church or ministry. Never trust items made by people who claim they have the ability to make such items or items that are packaged in new age bookstores or botanicas. This only contributes to the demonic problems.

Most priests will be more than happy to bless items for you. Another powerful method of protection is the Saint Benedict medal or crucifix. I can attest to the power this item has by the following story.

A friend of mine who is still involved in the new age (I've tried and still am trying to convert her) was having some issues with an entity she encountered while doing a supposed cleansing on a home. She asked me what to do, and I gave her a Saint Benedict crucifix.

She told me that she took the crucifix home and placed it on a table as she hadn't had time to hang it up. That night she had a small party at her apartment with a group of witches and Wiccans. (I didn't know it at the time, but this group was trying to recruit her.) She later called me to say that the witches who visited her apartment were upset when they saw the crucifix and especially the Saint Benedict medal on it. They said it gave them the creeps and demanded that it be removed immediately. My friend refused, and all of the witches left. They still have not contacted my friend nor made any attempt to recruit her. The particular crucifix I gave her was *not* blessed, but it still drove away these evil people along with their evil intentions! Praise Jesus!

Demonic Possession

Demonic possession is rare unless done voluntarily as in religions such as Voodoo and Santería. In these religions it is customary to invite the spirits to possess you.

When possession does occur it usually involves someone in the occult. Demons can gain entry into the human body by two known ports, one on the back of the neck and the other by way of the abdomen.

Possession occurs when a person gives a demon free will to control the body. Most people possessed by demons attempt suicide or murder in the last stages of possession as this is what the demon wants: to destroy humans.

Here are the indications or signs of demonic possession:

• Negative reaction to holy objects

• Strength beyond the capabilities of a normal person

• Knowledge of foreign or unknown languages

• Ability to predict future events or know hidden facts

Please keep in mind that possession is rare.

It's interesting to note that the devil and his minions cannot take control of one's soul; they can only control one's body.

If you believe that you or someone else is possessed or that your home is demonically infested, pray and stay in God's grace. Also contact a priest or a Catholic Charismatic Renewal Center. If you feel you're not getting the answers you deserve from clergy or your request for a house blessing is refused, seek help by contacting a Renewal Center.

I'm in the process of offering support and assistance to those who have loved ones involved in the occult and those who are victimized by the demonic. You can contact me at my ministry website at: www.stmichaelministry.com.

CHAPTER 26

PRAYERS

Before getting into prayers, I'd like to discuss the act of deliverance. Deliverance is basically a mini-exorcism. The act of performing the deliverance is usually done by clergy or lay people who are knowledgeable in such endeavors. Just like the power to heal, Jesus gave everyone the ability to "cast out" demons (Mark 16:17).

Knowing how to protect yourself is vital. Deliverance works for *all* evil spirits, not just those related to the occult. There are evil spirits that cause problems in humans such as hate, anger, jealousy, lust, etc. These spirits can enter a person through sins, life circumstances, or inheritance. Until they're driven out, they can continue to cause problems. If someone has had lasting emotional or mental problems, has had lasting sexual problems, or has been involved with cults or the occult, they are prime candidates for deliverance.

The first step in seeking deliverance is to recognize that you need it and give yourself to Jesus. Next is binding, casting out, and renouncing the evil spirits and demons, then claiming victory over Satan and his minions. Next, you must forgive yourself, God, and others. This starts the healing process. Healing prayer is usually done after a successful deliverance. Deliverance sessions may take several times because not all demons leave on the first try. Finally, you must lead a good spiritual life through prayer and going to mass and church. If you fail to do this, the demonic will come back stronger than they were before. You should be constantly on guard as the demonic will try to reenter. This usually happens by the demonic trying to influence your thoughts and emotions. Always remain vigilant and practice good spiritual warfare tactics such as the armor of God.

General Prayers

The following prayers are effective in defeating the evil one and his minions. The Blessed Mother and saints are helpful as well. When you pray, talk to whomever you're praying to just as you would a friend or family member. This intimate form of communication between you and those of heaven is most appreciated by them, and after a while the graces really start flowing.

Following are many prayers I hope you find useful.

Prayer for Settling a Haunting or Infestation

Lord Jesus, please put these spirits at rest and at peace. Please drive out any evil spirit or demon or satanic influence. I bind these and send them to the foot of your cross for you to send them back. Amen.

Our Father

Our Father, who art in heaven, hallowed be thy name, thy kingdom come, thy will be done on earth as it is in heaven. Give us this day our daily bread and forgive us our trespasses as we forgive those who trespass against us, and lead us not into temptation but deliver us from evil. Amen.

Hail Mary

Hail, Mary, full of grace the Lord is with thee: blessed art thou among women, and blessed is the fruit of thy womb,

Jesus. Holy Mary, Mother of God, pray for us sinners, now, and at the hour of our death. Amen.

Long Live Jesus

When tormented by the devil or tempted by him, Padre Pio would say, "Long live Jesus!" This would stop the torment and prevent preternatural events from occurring. Padre Pio would use this in order to determine if an apparition was holy in nature, or if it was simply the devil playing another trick. I've successfully used this several times.

Glory Be

Glory be to the Father, and to the Son, and to the Holy Spirit. As it was in the beginning, is now, and ever shall be, world without end. Amen.

Simple Guardian Angel Prayer

Everyone has been assigned a guardian angel to protect and guide them throughout this life and into the next. Saint Padre Pio was constantly communicating with his, as well as sending it wherever he wanted. You can do the same by asking your guardian angel to go to God, Jesus, the Blessed Mother, saints, or other guardian angels for help. Here is a simple prayer that they adore:

Angel of God, my guardian dear, to whom his love commits me here, ever this day (or night) be at my side, to light and guard, to rule and guide. Amen.

Prayer to Saint Michael

Saint Michael the Archangel, defend us in battle, be our protection against the wickedness and snares of the devil; may God rebuke him, we humbly pray; and do thou, O Prince of the Heavenly Host, by the divine power of God, cast into hell Satan and all the evil spirits who wander throughout the world seeking the ruin of souls. Amen.

Chaplet of Saint Michael

The Chaplet of Saint Michael is similar to the rosary. You can find one at any Catholic bookstore, or you can order one from my ministry: www.stmichaelministry.com. The instructions for praying the chaplet will be included with your purchase and are on my ministry website as well. This is a strong prayer to Saint Michael, the archangels, and the nine choirs. I pray the chaplet all the time. Once, I had a friend who had a terminal illness. I told them that I would pray for them but didn't tell them that I was praying the chaplet. After praying the chaplet, I received a phone call from them telling me that they saw strong angels around them, and the angels told my friend that I had sent them there! I've had several experiences like this. Be certain to include Saint Michael, the archangels, and the nine choirs in your prayers!

Invocation of the Nine Choirs of Angels

This is a great prayer as well! Use this if you don't have a Chaplet of Saint Michael.

O holy angels, watch over us at all times during this perilous life.

O holy archangels, be our guides on the way to heaven.

O heavenly choir of the principalities, govern us in soul and body.

O mighty powers, preserve us against the wiles of the demons.

O celestial virtues, give us strength and courage in the battle of life.

O powerful dominions, obtain for us dominion over the rebellion of our flesh.

O sacred thrones, grant us peace with God and man.

O brilliant cherubim, illuminate our minds with heavenly knowledge.

O burning seraphim, enkindle in our hearts the fire of charity. Amen.

The Armor of God

Much like the knights who wore armor to protect themselves in battle, you should wear your spiritual armor to protect yourself from the devil and his demons. Ephesians 6:10–18 describes the armor of God. While saying the prayer below, it helps to visualize "putting on" each item.

Lord God, I am putting on your armor to protect me from the evil one. I'm putting on the helmet of salvation to protect my mind from evil or negative thoughts or feelings, but Lord God, I'm also adding the blinders to protect my eyes from sin. Lord God, I want to stay on your straight and narrow path. I do not want to look left or right where there could be sin. If sin comes directly in front of me, Lord God, let my eyes look away. Lord God, I am now putting on the chest plate of righteousness to protect my heart, my soul, and the rest of my organs from evil or negative thoughts, feelings, or actions. Lord God, I am fastening the belt of truth around my waist so I know when the truth is being told to me or if it is a lie from Satan. I myself will tell the truth. Lord God, I am putting on the footgear so that I will be able to spread the great Gospel of peace. Lord God, I also carry the shield of faith for when Satan shoots his flaming arrows at me, they will be extinguished and be of no harm to me. Lord God, I carry the sword of the Holy Spirit, the Word of God, for nothing can defeat it, for the Word of God is the absolute truth. Amen.

Consecration to Saint Michael

Oh most Noble Prince of the Angelic Hierarchies, valorous warrior of Almighty God, and zealous lover of his glory, terror of the rebellious angels, and love and delight of all the just ones, my beloved Archangel Saint Michael, desiring to be numbered among your devoted servants, I, today offer and consecrate myself to you, and place myself, my family, and all I possess under your most powerful protection. I entreat you not to look at how little, I, as your servant have to offer, being only a wretched sinner, but to gaze, rather, with favorable eye at the heartfelt affection with which this offering is made, and remember that if from this day onward I am under your patronage, you must during all my life assist me, and procure for me the pardon of my many grievous offenses, and sins, the grace to love with all my heart my God, my dear Savior Jesus, and my Sweet Mother Mary, and obtain for me all the help necessary to arrive at my crown of glory. Defend me always from my spiritual enemies, particularly in the last moments of my life. Come then oh Glorious Prince and succor me in my last struggle, and with your powerful weapon cast far from me into the infernal abyss that prevaricator and proud angel that one day you prostrated in the celestial battle. Saint Michael, defend us in our daily battle so that we may not perish in the last judgment. Amen.

Prayer to Defeat the Work of Satan

O Divine Eternal Father, in union with your Divine Son and the Holy Spirit, and through the Immaculate Heart of Mary, I beg you to destroy the power of your greatest enemy—the evil spirits. Cast them into the deepest recesses of hell and chain them there forever! Take possession of your kingdom, which you have created and which is rightfully yours. Heavenly

Father, give us the reign of the Sacred Heart of Jesus and the Immaculate Heart of Mary. I repeat this prayer out of pure love for you with every beat of my heart and with every breath I take. Queen of Heaven! Sovereign Mistress of the angels! You who from the beginning have received from God the power and mission to crush the head of Satan, we humbly beseech you to send your holy legions, that, under your command and by your power, they may pursue the evil spirits, encounter them on every side, resist their bold attacks, and drive them hence into the abyss of eternal woe. Amen.

Prayer against Every Evil

Spirit of our God, Father, Son, and Holy Spirit, most Holy Trinity, Immaculate Virgin Mary, angels, archangels, and saints of heaven, descend upon us. Please purify us, Lord, mold us, fill us with yourself, use us. Banish all the forces of evil from us, destroy them, vanquish them, so that we can be healthy and do good deeds. Banish from us all spells, witchcraft, black magic, malefice, ties, maledictions, and the evil eye; diabolic infestations, oppressions, possessions; all that is evil and sinful, jealousy, perfidy, envy; physical, psychological, moral, spiritual, diabolical ailments. Burn all these evils in hell, that they may never again touch us or any other creature in the entire world. I command and bid all the power who molest me—by the power of God all powerful, in the name of Jesus Christ our savior, through the intercession of the Immaculate Virgin Mary—to leave us forever, and to be consigned into the everlasting hell, where they will be bound by Saint Michael the Archangel, Saint Gabriel, Saint Raphael, our guardian angels, and where they will be crushed under the heel of the Immaculate Virgin Mary. Amen.

Saint Benedict Prayer for Protection

Good Jesus, Saint Benedict believed in excelling and doing his very best to honor you. When he attended school, the undisciplined attitude of the other students dismayed him. Later, when he founded twelve monasteries, the demand for spiritual excellence in his monastic rule was so frustrating to lazy monks, some of them tried to poison him, but he blessed the drink and consumed it with no ill effects. I ask him to pray for the protection of my family, my church, and my friendships against the wickedness of Satan. Teach us, O Lord, to use your cross to conquer the evil in our world today. Saint Benedict, pray for us. Amen.

Prayer to Stop Demonic Infestation of a Household

In the name of Lord Jesus Christ, strengthened by the intercession of the Immaculate Virgin Mary, Mother of God, of Blessed Michael the Archangel, of the Blessed Apostles Peter and Paul, and all the angels and saints of heaven, and powerful in the holy authority of his name, and by my authority as head of the household, I (we) come before you, Heavenly Father, to ask you to come against the powers of darkness causing (name symptom or symptoms). Come against these powers, O Lord, because of the power of my (our) union with the Lord Jesus Christ. According to your Word, O Lord, and through His precious blood, I (we) resist the devil and his minions. I (we) resist the devil and all of his workers by the power of the Lord Jesus Christ. I (we) submit myself and submit this household to the Lordship and control of the Lord Jesus, and I (we) ask you, Father, to bring the power of my (our) Lord's incarnation, his glorification, and his second coming, directly to focus against all evil forces and all of the evil work against (insert address, item, etc.). By the authority of my position as head of the household, I (we) claim my (our) union with the Lord Jesus Christ, and I (we) resist the devil; I (we) resist the devil and his minions, and I (we) ask you, Heavenly Father, to force these evil ones to flee from before the truth of God.

Further, O Lord, I (we) ask you to bind together the whole kingdom of the evil one and to bind them from working, and finally to command all evil forces and their kingdom to leave (insert address, item, etc.) and to go where the Lord Jesus Christ may send them. Amen.

Curse Breakers and Deliverance Prayers

If you have a deliverance ministry in your area you should use them. The deliverance process listed here should be used by two people: one saying the prayers and the victim repeating the prayers. The other person assisting you should be of strong Christian faith and have been baptized in the Holy Spirit. If there is no deliverance ministry in your area and you know no one that meets these qualifications, then you can use self-deliverance. First, you should give yourself totally to Jesus and accept him as your savior. You can do this simply by a heartfelt prayer. Also confess your sins to him. Next, you should forgive anyone who hurt you, then forgive yourself. Forgiveness is an important part of this process as it closes the doors so that the demons cannot reenter. Even if you only forgive a little bit in the beginning, this will open the door for more forgiveness at a later time. Finally, before we get into this section it is a good idea at this point to get a pencil and paper and write down all of those occult sins (such as I held a séance, I participated in Wicca rituals, etc.) that you want to seek deliverance for. Put some strong thought into this as you'll use this information later in the following prayers. You should also add more things that you have a problem with, such as lust, gambling, anger, jealousy, etc. Be sure to write down any new age energy techniques as well as any new age religion.

You also need to clean house. Get rid of everything pertaining to the occult! These unwanted items should be burned or turned over to a deliverance ministry for destruction. Make sure these items are destroyed or turned over to ministry before doing the binding, deliverance, or renunciation prayers. (Some ministries do this in reverse, which is OK, but I am assuming that this is your first time doing this and that there aren't any deliverance ministries in your area.) Also, please don't resell these items or give them away. They must be destroyed and out of your life! By reselling or giving these things away, you're merely handing the demonic over to someone else. This may strengthen the demonic's hold on you.

Although some of these prayers may be repetitive, I've tried to cover all bases and leave no stone—or demon, for that matter—unturned. I've tried to provide the prayers to be said by the victim in case there isn't access to a deliverance ministry.

Curses can only be broken through prayer. Curses are totally the evil one's work. Therefore, you can't fully break a curse by using magic or any other methods controlled by him! Only through prayer!

You will need to repeat each of the following prayers three times: once for the Father, once for the Son, and last for the Holy Spirit. By doing this you are reclaiming victory from Satan's clutches for yourself as Satan loves to mock the Trinity and hates it.

Remember while doing these prayers that the Lord is always and will always be more powerful than Satan.

Finally, if you have a deliverance ministry in your area, you should use them. Follow the specific order mentioned below for the deliverance prayers. Before using the curse breakers, you should go to confession to clear your heart, or if you are not Catholic, simply confess your sins to Jesus through prayer. Pay close attention to any sin you may have committed against the originator of the curse if you believe they sent you the curse. If you feel that someone used one of your personal belongings to put the curse on you, you should renounce this object, so be sure to write it down as well. If you are having problems finding what to write down, these thoughts usually come to you faster when the Prayer for Discernment is recited. This prayer can also be recited by prayer ministers to find renunciations to use for the victim. You can use the Prayer for Discernment before the renunciation to find other items to renounce.

You should end with a prayer asking Jesus to heal you and fill those spaces that were occupied by the demonic with the Holy Spirit and Jesus's precious blood.

Following are the curse breaker prayers and the Prayer for Discernment, as well as the breaking satanic covenants prayer.

Prayer for Discernment

O Lord, I do not know what to ask you. You alone know my real needs and you love me more than I even know how to love. Enable me to discern my true needs, which are hidden from me. I ask for neither cross nor consolation: I wait in patience for you. My heart is open to you. For your great mercy's sake, come to me and help me. Put your mark on me and heal me, cast me down and raise me up. Silently I adore your holy will and your inscrutable ways. I offer myself in sacrifice to you and put all my trust in you. I desire only to do your will. Teach me how to pray and pray in me. Amen.

Prayer for Breaking Curses with Psalm 91

Repeat three times.

Father, I ask you first to forgive me for my sins and cleanse me from any area where I have allowed the devil to enter my life. I renounce any involvement with the works of darkness. In the name of Jesus, I now cancel every curse, and Father, I ask you to forgive the people who have spoken them against me. I thank you that those curses will no longer operate against me. In Jesus's name, they are broken right now, by the power of Almighty God. I cancel every evil that was spoken against me and ask you to cover me and my family with your protection according to your word in Psalm 91.

Then repeat Psalm 91.

Psalm 91

Repeat three times.

He who dwells in the shelter of the Most High will rest in the shadow of the Almighty. I will say of the Lord, "He is my refuge and my fortress, my God, in whom I trust." Surely he will save you from the fowler's snare and from the deadly pestilence. He will cover you with his feathers, and under his wings you will find refuge; his faithfulness will be your shield and rampart. You will not fear the terror of night, nor the arrow that flies by day, nor the pestilence that stalks in the darkness, nor the plague that destroys at midday. A thousand may fall at your side, ten thousand at your right hand, but it will not come near you. You will only observe with your eyes and see the punishment of the wicked. If you make the Most High your dwelling, then even the Lord, who is my refuge, then no harm will befall you, no disaster will come near your tent. For he will command his angels concerning you to guard you in all your ways; they will lift you up in their hands, so that you will not strike your foot against a stone. You will tread upon the lion and the cobra; you will trample the great lion and the serpent. "Because he loves me," says the Lord, "I will rescue him; I will protect him, for he acknowledges my name. He will call upon me, and I will answer him; I will be with him in trouble, I will deliver him and honor him. With long life will I satisfy him and show him my salvation." Amen.

Prayer to Be Freed from a Curse

Repeat three times.

Lord Jesus Christ, I believe you are the Son of God and the only way to God, that you died on the cross for my sins and for me. You were resurrected from the dead. I believe with what you did for me as my foundation that the vindications of Satan against me have been canceled by your cross. Therefore, Lord Jesus, I entrust myself to you. Because of this I oppose any malignant force of darkness that in any way has come into my life, either by my own acts, or by acts of my family or ancestors or any other thing that I was not aware of. Wherever there may be any shadows in my life, any malignant forces, I now renounce them, Lord. I refuse to submit to them any longer, and, in the mighty name of Jesus, the Son of God, I sit in judgment over all the forces of evil that torment me. I detach myself from them and absolutely free myself from their power. I call on the Holy Spirit of God to take me over, completely and absolutely, freeing me and detaching me from evil as only the Spirit of God can do. In the name of Jesus Christ. Amen.

Prayer to Be Freed from a Curse Sent by Another Person

Repeat three times.

Heavenly Father, I come to you regarding the evil that I believe has been sent against me by (state name of person/people if known). I confess any sins that I have committed related to this person, specifically (mention specific occult sins or wrongdoings). In the name of Jesus Christ, I forgive this person and anyone else who may have tried to harm me in any way, and I ask you, Lord, to carry out justice in this matter. I repent from any fear that I have allowed to influence me related to this evil. I turn from my sin and ask to be cleansed from it by faith in Jesus Christ, by his precious shed blood in every level of my life, body, soul, and spirit.

In the name of Jesus Christ, and by his authority, I cancel every hex, curse, spell, ungodly prayers, vortexes, and satanic assignments that have been made against me and my family. I break any curses associated with black magic, witchcraft, Voodoo, Santería, or any other form of evil. Heavenly Father, I ask that you would reverse any damage that has been caused in my life or in my family's life as a result of the evil that was sent to me. I pray for your healing and restoration in our lives.

If any personal belongings or contact objects have been used in directing this evil against me, I renounce ownership to such things and ask you, Father, to sever any and all ties between me and those items. Jesus Christ, please cover myself and my family with your precious blood, and please place a thick hedge of protection around us to stop any further attacks of evil. Thank you Father! I pray in the name of Jesus Christ. Amen.

Prayer to Break Satanic Covenants

Repeat three times.

I renounce ever signing my name over to Satan or having my name signed over to Satan. I announce and proclaim that my name is written in the Lamb's Book of Life. I renounce any ceremony in which I may have been wed to Satan, and I announce that I am the Bride of Christ. I renounce all satanic assignments, covenants, pacts, and dedications that I made with Satan, or that were made for me. I announce that I am a partaker of the new covenant with Christ. I reject and renounce all curses and assignments made for me for the service of Satan. I renounce (anything you specifically remember!). I trust only in the precious shed blood of my Lord Jesus Christ and what he accomplished on the cross. I look to the Holy Spirit for guidance. I renounce all guardians and surrogate parents assigned to me by Satanists. I renounce all baptisms, rituals, or teachings by Satanists. I announce that I have been baptized into Jesus Christ and my identity is now in Christ. I renounce and reject all Satanists. I renounce and reject all demons and familiar spirits attached to any part of me by Satanists. I reject all spirit guides assigned to my other than holy angels. I announce that God is my Heavenly Father and the Holy Spirit is my guardian. By this, I am sealed until the day of my redemption. I will accept only God's assignment for me. In the name of Jesus Christ, amen.

Binding, Renouncements, Deliverance, and Victory Prayers

The following prayers need to be said in a specific order. First is the binding prayer. After completion, this will give distance to the oppression and problems caused by the demonic. Following the binding prayer is Psalm 35:1–10, then the direct renouncements (using those items you wrote earlier, such as fear, hate, etc.). Finally the deliverance and victory prayers are prayed. The best-case scenario would be to have deliverance ministers carry out these prayers; however, as a lot of people don't have a deliverance ministry close, I've modified these to be said by the person affected. If you have to stop while reciting these prayers, you draw a blank, or cannot say them, this is Satan trying to distract you. You may find that if the devil has a tight hold on you, you may not be able to say these at all. Ask another person to assist you by reading the prayers and repeat after them. You should then start contacting churches in your area to locate a deliverance ministry. These prayers are very powerful, and most people shouldn't have any problems.

Binding Prayer Number One

Repeat three times. You can use this as a group prayer by altering it slightly!

> In the name of Jesus, I bind you spirit of (insert word you wrote down, such as anger, jealousy, lust, Ouija board, tarot cards) and I cast you out sending you to the foot of the cross of Jesus so he can deal with you accordingly. I take authority that is mine as a Christian and in the name of Jesus Christ I bind any power of the spirit of the air, water, fire, satanic forces of nature, or the underground and the netherworld itself. I bind them in the name of Jesus Christ, and I forbid any demonic harassment, demonic interplay, or communications. In the name of Jesus Christ, I bind all confusion, interruption, and spirit of the occult. I bind all distraction in Jesus's name. I bind all lust in Jesus's name and any spirit, power, or force that is opposed to Jesus Christ. I rebuke in the name of Jesus Christ any satanic prayers, curses, hexes, or spells sent against me, and I decommission every demon sent to implement them against me. I send every spirit not of our Lord directly and immediately to the cross of Jesus to do only the will of Jesus. I cover myself with the blood of Jesus and also my family and loved ones. All of you angels and saints of God, I invite you to be present with us, fill this place and surround us this day. Minister to us and with us. Amen.

Binding Prayer Number Two

Repeat three times.

> In the name of Jesus, I bind you spirit of (name you wrote down) and I cast you out sending you to the foot of the cross of Jesus so he can deal with you accordingly. Heavenly Father, we come before you, trusting in Christ's payment for us, and we ask that you would bind and gag all evil spirits and forces of darkness in, near, and around us, so that they may

not interfere with us now. We acknowledge that you are the Ruler: "Far above all principality and power and might and dominion, and every name that is named, not only in this age but also in that which is to come." You have told us, in your faithfulness, "I will give you the keys of the kingdom of heaven; whatever you bind on earth will be bound in heaven, and whatever you loose on earth will be loosed in heaven." We claim our position with you, through your grace, and ask that as it is written, so it be done. In the name of the Lord Jesus Christ we ask and in faith we receive. Amen.

Psalm 35:1–10

Pray for immediate deliverance.

Oppose, O Lord, those who oppose me; war upon those who make war upon me. Take up the shield and buckler; rise up in my defense. Brandish lance and battle-ax against my pursuers. Say to my soul, "I am your salvation." Let those who seek my life be put to shame and disgrace. Let those who plot evil against me be turned back and confounded. Make them like chaff before the wind, with the angel of the Lord driving them on. Make their way slippery and dark, with the angel of the Lord pursuing them. Without cause they set their snare for me; without cause they dug a pit for me. Let ruin overtake them unawares; let the snare they have set catch them; let them fall into the pit they have dug. Then I will rejoice in the Lord, exult in God's salvation. My very bones shall say, "O Lord, who is like you? Who rescue the afflicted from the powerful, the afflicted and needy from the despoiler?"

Direct Renouncements

Use the items you wrote before and insert them as needed. Repeat three times.

> In the name of Jesus Christ, I take authority and I renounce the spirit of (insert word you wrote down/strong emotion). I break your power and close the door so you cannot reenter, and I send you to the foot of the cross of Jesus.

Prayer for Deliverance

Repeat three times.

> My Lord, you are all powerful, you are God, you are Father. We beg you through the intercession and help of the archangels Michael, Raphael, and Gabriel, for the deliverance of (insert victim's name) and our brothers and sisters who are enslaved by the evil one. All saints of heaven, come to our aid. From anxiety, sadness, and obsessions, we beg you, free us, O Lord. From hatred, fornication, and envy, we beg you, free us, O' Lord. From thoughts of jealousy, rage, and death, we beg you, free us, O Lord. From every thought of suicide and abortion, we beg you, free us, O Lord. From the onslaught of this sniper, we beg you, free us, O Lord. From every form of sinful sexuality, we beg you, free us, O Lord. From every division in our family, and every harmful friendship, we beg you, free us, O Lord. From every sort of spell, malefice, witchcraft, and every form of the occult and homicide, we beg you, free us, O Lord. Lord, you who said, "I leave you peace, my peace I give you," grant that through the intercession of the Virgin Mary, we may be liberated from every evil spell and enjoy your peace always. In the name of Christ, our Lord. Amen.

Renunciation of Satan and Claiming the Full Victory

From the Order of the Legion of Saint Michael. Repeat three times.

Satan, I renounce you and all your works, including all and whatsoever witchcraft, Voodoo, Spiritism, tarot cards, and everything that directly or disguised might have any connection with you. I renounce any connection that I or members of my family, friends, and acquaintances may have had with your works. I renounce you, Satan, in the name of Jesus Christ I order you to leave me now, in the name of Jesus Christ, the Son of the living God, my savior.

I claim the full victory that my Lord Jesus Christ won on the cross for me. Having disarmed the powers and authorities, He made a public spectacle of them, triumphing over them by the cross. His victory for me is my victory. In the name of the Lord Jesus Christ I renounce all the workings of Satan in my life in all its forms, whether brought into my life by my actions or by others'. I break all attachments, ground, curses, spells, and rights Satan may have in my life whether such ground was gained through my actions or through others. Strengthened by the intercession of the Immaculate Virgin Mary, Mother of God, of Blessed Michael the Archangel, of the Blessed Apostles Peter and Paul, and all the angels and saints of heaven, and powerful in the holy authority of the name of the Lord Jesus Christ, I ask you, Lord, to command Satan and all his minions, whomever they may be, to get out of my life and stay out. With that authority I now take back the ground in my life for Christ. I now dedicate myself to the Lord Jesus Christ; I belong to Him alone. Amen.

Renunciation of Satan and Occult Activity Claiming Full Victory

Repeat three times.

I claim the full victory that my Lord Jesus Christ won on the cross for me. Having disarmed the powers and authorities, He made a public spectacle of them, triumphing over them by the cross.

I have been involved in the occult sins of (insert occult sins). I renounce these sins and the use of my body in conjunction with them. I confess the occult sins of my ancestors including (insert ancestors' occult sins, if any, or skip). I renounce the past sins of my ancestors and any unknown sins that they committed. I apply the blood of Jesus Christ to these sins and break any curses that may have come down the generations to me or the rest of my family.

In the name of the Lord Jesus Christ, I renounce the workings of Satan and his demons in my life in all their forms, whether brought into my life by me or by others.

I break all attachments, ground, curses, spells, and rights Satan may have in my life whether such ground was gained through my actions or through other's.

I now take my position as a redeemed child of the Immaculate Virgin Mary, the Blessed Saint Michael the Archangel, the Blessed Apostles Peter and Paul, and the angels and saints of heaven, in the holy authority of the Lord Jesus Christ, I ask you, Lord, to command Satan and all his minions, whomever they may be, to get out of my life and stay out. With that authority I now take back the ground in my life gained by Satan through my sins. I reclaim this ground and my life for Christ. I now dedicate myself to the Lord Jesus Christ. I belong to Him alone.

Jesus, please cleanse me with your blood and fill me afresh with the Holy Spirit. I want to receive the Holy Spirit now. (Pause for silent prayer to accept the Holy Spirit.) Please unite my heart to live for you in righteousness. I am your vessel, Lord. Thanks you! Amen.

Sacramentals

Saint Benedict Medal

The Saint Benedict Medal is a strong protective medal available at any Catholic bookstore. You may also order one from my ministry: www.stmichaelministry.com. Have a priest bless the medal before you wear it.

Blessed Salt

This is salt that is blessed by a priest. It's good for sprinkling around an infested home and can even be eaten by someone under demonic influence.

Blessed Oil

Blessed oil is used for anointing someone or objects. It's effective because the beginning of the blessing includes the prayer of exorcism.

Holy Water

Holy water is available by request at any Catholic church. Use it for sprinkling on objects or persons and around rooms that are infested.

REFERENCES AND RECOMMENDATIONS

Ashcraft, Rev. Jack. *Ecclesiae Militantis: A Course in Spiritual Warfare and Exorcism*. Self-published, CreateSpace, 2013.

Ashcraft, Rev. Jack. *The Real Exorcist: Spiritual Warfare Methodology*. Self-published, CreateSpace, 2013.

Blai, Adam C. *Hauntings, Possessions, and Exorcisms*. Steubenville, OH: Emmaus Road Publishing, 2014.

Boyd, Katie. *Demons and Demonology in the 21st Century*. Atglen, PA: Schiffer Publishing, 2009.

Fiore, Edith. *The Unquiet Dead: A Psychologist Treats Spirit Possession*. New York: Ballantine Books, 1987.

Haggart, G. P. *Mechanics of Demonology*. Self-published, Lulu, 2010.

Haggart, G. P. *Mechanics of Demonology*. Vol. 2, *The Intermediate Level*. Self-published, CreateSpace, 2013.

Hampsch, Rev. John H. *How to "Raze" Hell: Strategies of Spiritual Warfare*. Goleta, CA: Queenship Publishing Company, 1997.

Hawkins, Craig S. *Witchcraft: Exploring the World of Wicca*. Grand Rapids, MI: Baker Books, 1996.

Kail, Tony M. *A Cop's Guide to Occult Investigations: Understanding Satanism, Santeria, Wicca, and Other Alternative Religions*. Boulder, CO: Paladin Press, 2003.

Linedecker, Clifford L. *Hell Ranch: The Nightmare Tale of Voodoo, Drugs, and Death in Matamoros.* Austin, TX: Diamond Books, 1989.

Lozano, Neal. *Resisting the Devil: A Catholic Perspective on Deliverance.* Huntington, IN: Our Sunday Visitor, 2010.

Mather, George A., and Larry A. Nichols. *A Dictionary of Cults, Sects, Religions, and the Occult.* Grand Rapids, MI: Zondervan Publishing House, 1993.

Mathews, Chris. *Modern Satanism: Anatomy of a Radical Subculture.* Westport, CT: Praeger Publishers, 2009.

Palagruto, Anne. *Deliver Us from Evil: A Guide to Spiritual Warfare and Exorcism.* Philadelphia: TPA Publishing, 2004.

Shepard, Leslie. *How to Protect Yourself against Black Magic and Witchcraft.* Secaucus, NJ: Citadel Press, 1978.

FATHER ROOKEY DEDICATION

It is with great sadness that while writing this book, I have learned of the passing of one of the key people responsible for helping me out of the dark world of the occult. Father Peter Mary Rookey was born October 12, 1916. He was internationally known as the "healing priest." Father Rookey had his first contact with the gift of healing as a young boy when a firecracker exploded in his face, blinding him. Doctors said nothing could be done to save his sight. His mother prayed for the Lord to heal him and prayed the rosary at night. Within a year his sight was fully restored. He then entered the priesthood.

Father Rookey held his first healing service in 1948 while blessing people after Mass at the Servite priory he helped found in Northern Ireland. Some of the people he blessed came back and said they had been healed.

Father Rookey returned to the United States in the late 1980s at Our Lady of Sorrows. The Servite Order was seeking to restore the Church to its original prominence and asked Father to resume his healing services. Father Rookey continued to do so, carrying out his work in his ministry, known as the International Compassion Ministry. There have been many miracles and healings reported.

Father Rookey passed away as he slept on September 9–10, 2014. He was ninety-seven years old.

Regardless of the hour of day, Father Rookey still had time to pray with you, and his door was always open for a visit. He *always* had the time for anyone, regardless of what other things were going on in his life and ministry. He helped both me and my family tremendously throughout the years and touched the lives of many people.

Goodbye, Father, you'll be missed.

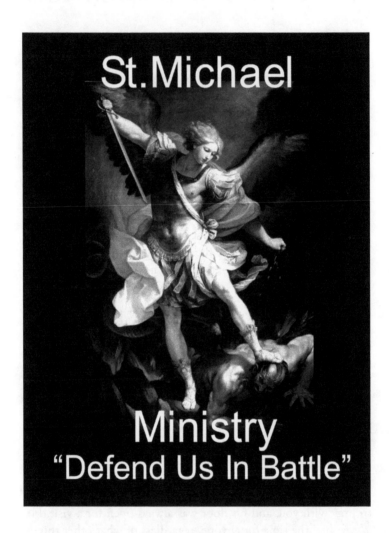

To purchase St. Michael Chaplets, St. Benedict medals, or for more information, visit our website at: www.stmichaelministry.com